7 Steps to Sales Scripts for B2B Appointment Setting

Creating Cold Calling Phone Scripts for Business to Business Selling, Lead Generation and Sales Closing.

A Primer for Appointment Setters

Scott Channell

Also by Scott Channell

Setting Sales Appointments: How to Gain Access to Top Level Decision Makers

Published by New Mark Press.
April 2013

ISBN: 978-0-9765241-9-9

All brand names and product names used in this book are trademarks, registered trademarks, or trade names of their respective holders.

This publication is designed to provide accurate and authoritative information with regard to the subject matter covered. It is sold with the understanding that the publisher is not engaged in rendering legal, accounting, or other professional advice. If legal advice or other expert assistance is required, the services of a qualified professional person should be sought.
- From a Declaration of Principles jointly adopted by a Committee of the American Bar Association and a Committee of Publishers and Associations.

This book is available at quantity discounts for bulk purchases. For information, call 978-296-2700

Scott Channell offers training, speaking and coaching programs.

For Information visit AccordingToScott.com

**For my daughters
Joanna and Kelly**

Table of Contents

Acknowledgments

Special acknowledgement must be given to Kim Nyland, one of the country's top B2B appointment setters. Kim is an expert on appointment setting and sales process. They say "you are who you hang around with." Working with Kim on many projects over the years has sharpened the concepts and samples presented here. I am very fortunate to be the beneficiary of her advice and wisdom.

Thank you to Morgan Chapman for not only his input on this manuscript, but for being such a great example of what can be accomplished when these principles are implemented. In one year Morgan coached his inside sales team from about 126 appointments set to 1,034 appointments set (75% at the C-Level) and 432 event registrations using the script principles in this book. Morgan possesses not only great sales knowledge, but the magic of being able to lead others to top performance. During the writing of this book, he passed on some of that magic to me and for that I am very grateful.

A big thank you to my editor, Gail Lowe and Ellyn Olson for cover design and book production.

Introduction

It's not unusual to spend hours laboring over the wording of a 30-second "set the appointment" script. Hours.

It can take that long to craft verbiage that makes buyers choke on the words "I'm all set" and want to listen to you more. A little more on the phone. Much more at a face-to-face meeting, a phone appointment, a webinar, an event.

To have impact, the type of impact that launches a sales process with a qualified buyer, you have to accept reality.

Before I started teaching others to set sales appointments I personally smiled and dialed my way to setting more than 2,000 C-Level sales appointments in many diverse industries.

Those appointments were set not because I did what I wanted, or what I was comfortable with, or what I wished would work.

Those appointments were set because I did what worked. Period. Regardless of my personal comfort .

Qualified leads are the life blood of high earnings and top performing teams. Many high earners and top performing teams use the phone effectively to get in front of high-probability high-worth buyers. The process is frustrating and a mystery to most but this is not rocket science.

Many use the phone effectively to set appointments with prospects, current and past clients, and referral sources. You can also.

These are the steps to creating scripts with impact. You have plenty of script samples and component examples to guide you.

Smile when you dial,
Scott Channell
AccordingToScott.com

Chapter 1

Communicating an "Exchange of Value."

Sales scripts.

Sales scripts that connect you to qualified buyers.

Sales scripts that convey your credibility and value.

Sales scripts that result in targeted high-value, high-probability buyers saying, "Yes, I will meet with you." Or, "Let's schedule that phone appointment," "I'll attend your webinar," or "I'll see you at the event."

Magic words that when uttered transform into closed deals without all that bother of selling.

Scripts that you could just start using to instantly turbo-charge your sales process.

Wish such things existed.

But they don't.

**More New Business.
Reactivate dormant accounts.
Sell more to current accounts.
Close those referred.
Get more referrals from those
who can send them.**

The script samples in this primer are illustrative of how you sell what is typically the "first step" of a higher level sales process. A meeting. That meeting might be in-person, over the phone, participation in a webinar or attendance at an event.

The bigger picture is that you are obtaining a commitment for an exchange of value. Their time, your information and expertise. This is the official launch of a sales process calculated to close deals.

Sell more meetings; you have more opportunities to close deals. It's that simple.

Too few meetings... *you'll find the Ramen in aisle 4.*

This script writing process and these script structures will help you achieve the following:

Meet with more top-level decision makers who can write checks.

Sell more to existing accounts.

Reactivate dormant or previous clients/accounts.

Meet with those that have been referred to you.

Connect with those who could refer qualified buyers to you.

The bottom line is that in each of these circumstances you greatly increase the chance of closing a deal if you can meet with someone now, rather than later.

Those that think of prospecting as solely about closing new business with strangers think too narrowly.

The same skill set and mindset that gets you in the door at the top level of targeted qualified prospects will enable you to sell more to current clients, previous accounts, those that are referred to you and generate more referrals.

For more script tips, samples and updates visit **www.AccordingToScott.com/script-extras**

Chapter 2

B2B vs B2C.

Does it matter?
Not really.

Again, this primer will use a B2B environment for illustration and script samples. But the same structures and concepts work in many B2C environments.

In fact, my very first "appointment setting" project, in the early 90's, was with a 30 seat telecenter that set appointments for a B2C home heating oil company throughout New England. That center is where I cut my teeth in appointment setting. They ended up setting more appointments in the slow time of year than they had previously in their busy time of year.

From there I went to an employee relocation company that needed to meet with CEO's/Presidents/ Executive level VP's of companies with more than 1,000 employees. They could close when they could get in the door. They just had to open more doors. Four expert consultants before me had tried and failed to set appointments for this company.

One exceptional consultant had the bright idea of creating a Hawaiian room. They spread sand around the phone room and employees took turns calling for appointments and competing for a Hawaiian vacation. That didn't work. Surprise.

Working a process of trial and error and error and error, I created a call process with scripts that ended up setting more than 500 qualified appointments for that company.

After that project I worked in many environments and went on to personally set more than 2,000 C-level sales appointments in diverse industries. Sitting in the cube, making the calls, not always smiling when I was dialing.

My point? The principles of success and script structures used to set appointments for a B2C home heating oil company were the same principles and structures that yielded setting 500 appointments in a B2B high-level, big company major-sales environment.

The same script structures worked across many diverse B2B call programs. Information technology, consulting, manufacturing, management services, publishing, communications, educational equipment, cleaning services, financial services, wealth management, logistics, insurance, software: The script structures that worked were remarkably similar.

Financial services, wealth management and insurance

products blur the lines between B2B and B2C. But in each environment it is the same script structures which get you in the door.

Strictly B2C environments? From home security systems to home repair, mortgages, to direct selling house parties, these same script structures have proven themselves over and over. They are not substantially different.

I have worked on many B2B and B2C campaigns with in-house teams and telecenters, even written scripts for incoming calls for some popular infomercials I would be ashamed to admit to. The core principles of how to achieve a business result using the phone are remarkably constant across all those environments.

Those in B2B environments that think they have nothing to learn from the B2C world, or vice versa, are sadly mistaken. It's all about effective communication in an environment where seconds count, every word matters and people's automatic reflex is to "just say no."

For more script tips, samples and updates visit
www.AccordingToScott.com/script-extras

Chapter 3

Magic Scripts.

Those who believe there are "magic scripts" floating about which, if captured and repeated, could turn on a faucet of sales appointments and qualified opportunities that would result in untold sales commissions and new accounts -- are walking among the clueless.

Why?
Three reasons.

First, sales scripts are important, yes. But good sales scripts are NEVER the only reason sales prospecting is successful. You must work a total process to be consistently successful at sales prospecting. Your sales scripts are at maximum 25% - 30% of that process. Without the rest of the process, your scripts are worth nothing.

"Good scripts" only help you if you are talking to enough of the "right people" at the right time. It is your overall process that will consistently deliver up those interactions.

What good is it to have a decent script if you are not talking to anybody worthwhile?

Own What You Say

Second, scripts that sell are specific to you and they emerge from a script creation process which enables you to truly own what you say.

Your company.
Your personal experience.
Your strengths.
Your region.
Your competitive environment.
Your business priorities.
Your points of competitive advantage.

Example: I do a lot of work for some major franchise companies. Franchisee to franchisee there can be variations in the scripts that work. Those variations typically emphasize strengths, experiences and business priorities of the individual master franchisee. Not all the winning scripts are exactly the same.

Example: Among companies that have many top producers, the scripts that work are not exactly alike. They tend to have similar components and structures, but they are not exactly alike with every salesperson. Again, there is room for variation based upon individual strengths and business objectives.

So, scripts that work are specific to you.

They are also the result of a script creation process that enables the caller, the salesperson, to own the words. You must own the words to deliver them with confidence and conviction.

To own the words you must have either gone through the script creation process outlined in this primer, or you must understand the component parts, the word choices within those component parts and the structure of a winning script to understand why a winning script works.

You need a few "ah ha" moments during the script creation process as to:

Component parts of a script that sells.

Your word and phrase choices within each component part.

The structure of a good script.

If you try to write a script and don't grasp the above, your script will be weak. If you try to deliver a script and don't grasp the above, you won't own the script. You won't deliver it with confidence and you will constantly try to deviate from it.

Adapt, Evolve, Rewrite

Third, scripts evolve.

Even when you follow this process to create a solid initial script, it will change. It is normal and expected for a script to be massaged and modified about 6 times before you determine you have it right.

That's right. Expect to modify your script 6 times before it reaches final form.

Now let's get into the actual preparation steps of writing "good scripts" that sell the typical first step (a meeting face-to-face, by phone, or attendance at a webinar or event) in many sales processes.

But first a few caveats...

There is a difference between a high-level and lower-level sales environment.

When I refer to scripts having some degree of flexibility I am referring much more to a high-level sales environment than I am a lower-level sales environment.

A high-level sales environment is typically higher investment, more risk, multiple steps, has multiple decision makers and a long sales cycle. A lower-level sales environment is typically more activity oriented. Stack 'em high, make 'em fly. Buy now. Next! Usually a smaller investment, less at stake, one decision maker, short cycle type sale.

Lower-level high volume sales environments tend to be more scripted, and they should be. What works tends to be proven over time by tracking and statistics. Plus, the skill sets of callers don't typically allow for flexibility.

In a lower-level environment, stick to the script.

Even in high-level environments, you have less flexibility up front.

It makes sense that in high-level environments, where there are more variables and nuances, that there should be more flexibility in sales scripts.

True, but there is less flexibility in the front of the script path than there is in the middle or toward the end of the script path.

What do I mean?

Let's take a 30 second script calculated to set an appointment. That will usually be about a 2 1/2 to 3 minute conversation. The deeper into that conversation you go the more flexibility you have for massaging and variation.

But the first 30 seconds. Sorry. Even in high-level sales environments you have virtually no room for adjustments.

Scripts are just preparation.

Frankly, I don't understand people who refuse to write down and then use telephone sales scripts.

It is incomprehensible to me that people would march into an environment where failure is the norm, where seconds count, where every word matters... and not be prepared.

That is what writing scripts is all about. Preparation. You identify repetitive scenarios, anticipate common responses, brainstorm all your possible word choices and select the words most likely to achieve your business objective.

Preparation. So that when you hear "hello?" you drastically increase the odds of achieving your business objective.

Few are so smart, or so personable....

Sorry, but those of you who refuse to write down the words most calculated to achieve your business objectives in repetitive situations, because you don't want to sound "scripted." You are letting a lot of money slip through your fingers.

"Sounding scripted" and using scripts are 2 totally different things. One has nothing to do with the other.

Do you really think that you are so witty, your personality so enchanting, your Hal 9000 intellect so superior that you can process each situation second by second and magically pull out of the air just the right things to say that accomplish your business objective?

Are you out of your mind? If you had the ability to magically anticipate the behavior of each individual who picked up the phone you wouldn't be prospecting.

It is much more likely that your naturally inspired verbiage waters down your value proposition and meanders like smoke to the ceiling. You choose words with less impact and squander time.

Sales prospecting on the phone does not have to turn you into a robot.

There is room for flexibility.
Top producers will vary their approach.
Among high producing sales teams there will be

variations in scripts.

But... but... but...

The similarities among all of those winning scripts are many.

It is not the differences that make all of them work. It is the similarities.

Whether you are setting an appointment, qualifying an opportunity, generating a lead, closing a sale, or building attendance to an event...

...there are reasons why good scripts tend to work and lousy scripts predict a macaroni and cheese diet.

For more script tips, samples and updates visit
www.AccordingToScott.com/script-extras

Chapter 4

Commonalities to Scripts That Work.

Time limitations.
Structure.
Component parts.
Clarity.
Use of super words.
Focus on buyers only.
Avoiding words and phrases that doom you.

All winning scripts have these things in common. Let's explore.

Brainstorm all words and phrases for each component part of your script.

As to each component part of your script you need to write down every possible option you have. The objective in the beginning is to brainstorm. Write down every thought you have. Don't worry about polish or length or even if it makes sense.

Many times you'll punch up your script with more value and impact by polishing a previous half baked thought or very long concept.

Write down everything you can think of.

When you do this, not only will you write better sales scripts for the telephone but you will be better prepared for your prospect meetings and end up closing more business. Why? Because you are better prepared.

Those with the most benefits that matter... win.

Example: Whenever I do a presentation I always interview a representative sample of salespeople. Among other questions... why do people/companies buy from you? What benefits do they get?

Typically an individual salesperson will max out with 5 or 6 benefits. Then it's, "Um.. Ahhhh.... I can't think of anything else." Typically every salesperson will mention 1 or 2 benefits not mentioned by the others. So if I interview four salespeople I typically get a list of 10-12 benefits. But individually, each salesperson could only think of 5 or 6.

When that same question is asked to the whole team during training, it is not unusual for 30 to 40 benefits to go on the board. I have had instances where teams come up with over 100 reasons why people buy from them.

Yet individually, the typical salesperson is hard

pressed to name more than 6 benefits their accounts get.

Who is likely to sell more?

Who writes better scripts?
Who is more prepared for prospect conversations and meetings?
Who is more likely to select the best words to convey value and credibility?
Who is more likely to move the process to a higher "next step?"
Who closes more business?

The person whose sales radar contains all the reasons why someone or a company may buy, or the salesperson whose sales radar is limited to about 6 reasons?

Let's brainstorm all word choices within each component part of your script.

There are 6 component parts of a set-the-appointment script.

1. Who you are and where you are calling from.

2. What you do.

3. Why you are credible.

4. The benefits people/companies get when buying from you.

5. The value you will deliver at the meeting. Note: You communicate the value you will deliver at the meeting -- not value only realized possibly at some nebulous time in the future if some contingencies

occur, which at the time of your call is unlikely.

6. You ask for the meeting.

7. Then you shut up.

For more script tips, samples and updates visit
www.AccordingToScott.com/script-extras

Chapter 5

The Best "Piles of Words" Gets the Meeting and the Close.

**Sales script preparation:
Step 1. Your name and your company.**

People's minds race 10X faster than you can talk. If they don't have clarity right up front as to who is calling from where and what you might do for them, their minds will wander and not focus on what you are saying.

So you might start...

"Hi, this is Scott Channell from ..."

Or,

"Hi, this is Scott from ..."
Should you use your last name?

Guiding principle: Ruthlessly rip out every unnecessary word. Start here. They will not initially remember or care about your last name. Delete it. Do so and you are 1 second closer to saying something that might matter.

From what company?

Again, you have strategic choices.

... from Biz-Pro...
... from Biz-Pro computer systems...
... from Biz-Pro business computers...

... from Mega Social Media
... from Mega Company

Most of the time simply stating your company name is sufficient.

But sometimes you need to make strategic adjustments.

Example: Let's take offerings that are overly common and everybody "thinks" they know what it is all about. They dig in with an emphatic "no" even before you can get to the meat of your pitch.

Social media and credit card processing immediately come to mind. People are barraged daily with these offers.

Many who are recipients of such calls, recognize them as social media or credit card processing pitches and shut down. Then they say "no." The call is over.

If you are a "better" social media or credit card processing company, you have a problem. If you can't get to the meat of your pitch, your credibility, your benefits and the value you will deliver statements... those who have a need you can fill and would consider meeting with you... have no way to distinguish you from the myriad of morons who contact them and waste their time. The call is over before you get there.

So "Mega Social Media" might become "Mega Company" in the front part of your script. It enables you to get deeper into your pitch and communicate some credibility and substance, so that qualified buyers won't in knee-jerk fashion jump to conclusions and devalue you.

Sales script preparation:
Step 2. What do you do?

Again, to have any chance of gaining a foothold into someone's mind over the phone, you must start by communicating who you are, where you are calling from and what you do. There must be clarity as to these three elements up front. Fail here and you are toast before you even begin.

Describing what you do is important not only to orient the suspect, but it is also where you begin the qualification process.

Those who use winning scripts focus on buyers only. Unlike the lost who write their scripts to have more comfortable conversations with those who will never buy... top producers want to immediately send a signal to potential buyers... here is something that may benefit you.

So top producers describe what they do with absolute clarity, so that buyers choke on the words, "We are all set" or "I'm busy. Gotta bounce."

This is where you start to give buyers "cause for pause."

Write down all the possible choices you have to describe what you do.

- We are a business computer company.
- We manage and install corporate IT systems.
- We keep corporate IT systems running.

Another example:

- We provide business technology solutions.
- We bring interactive technology into businesses.
- We specialize in integration of technology into corporations such as product X, program Y and brand Z.

You have choices. Write them all down.

Guiding principle: This statement should be plain, simple and direct. We do X. No fluff words such as best or superior. The trouble with fluff words at this stage is that people don't know enough to agree or disagree with you. It is only your opinion. You are asking them for a judgment. Don't do that. If you do, they will immediately start discounting what you say. Keep to simple statements of fact with no embellishment.

All you are shooting for is for them to think, "I get it." That's all.

Words of caution: Clarity is critical here. Simplicity wins. Many times when conducting script critiques the "what we do" component becomes very long and convoluted. The problem with that is that "buyers" can't grasp it. They don't understand what you do. So if you might solve a problem they have or improve their conditions in some way, nothing clicks in the minds of buyers. They say, "Wait a minute. Maybe I should listen to this. There may be something here for me."

If they can't grasp what you do, they are not listening to anything else you say. Even if you have great credibility, benefit and value components in your script, buyers are not really listening because they are trying to figure out what you do.

For more script tips, samples and updates visit
www.AccordingToScott.com/script-extras

Chapter 6

True Script Differentiation.

Sales script preparation:
Step 3. Your credibility statement.

If there is 1 missing link in losing scripts, 1 mistake I see commonly that absolutely cripples your ability to sell over the phone, it is this:

The lack of an effective credibility statement.
In fact, the lack of any credibility statement at all.

How do they know you are more worthwhile than the other 20 people who call them every week to waste their time?

How are people supposed to know that you are not some schmuck working out of their parents' basement?

How do people know you are unique and more valuable than others they might find with a few keystrokes online?

They don't.
They don't unless you tell them.

Why should they invest even a few moments on the phone with a stranger of unknown qualifications and experience when the identity of qualified vendors and experts are just a few keystrokes away?

They won't. Unless you give them reason to do so.

Example: I once received a call from a very accomplished sales leader in a niche industry. She was now consulting, and she could not understand why people were hesitant to meet with her and why so many appointments scheduled were canceled.

Here is a clue. People who blow you off obviously don't "get" your credibility or value.

In this case I knew a lot about the results that this salesperson had achieved for organizations. She had a stellar record of achievement helping companies solve common and costly problems. Prior to her consulting career she had been in the field and had consistently ranked within the top three of a 15,000+ sales organization.

Did the person she scheduled the phone appointments with know anything about the results she had achieved for other organizations?

No.

Did the person she scheduled the phone appointments with know anything about her extraordinary record of personal achievement in the industry before she started consulting?

No.

Should we really be surprised that decision makers blew her off or no-showed her appointments?

No.

Take a look at the credibility statements in the front half of the script that changed her life.

"Hi. This is Liz from Mega Industries. We help companies to _____ and those that have worked with us have achieved major benefit A, monster result B and significant achievement C. Before I started consulting I was a top performer in this industry achieving stellar result A, Super result B and unbelievable result C. ... continuing. "

Conveying credibility makes a huge difference and if you do not do so right up front, you are toast.

Let's take a look at some credibility statement options to get you thinking.

- Work with 3,000 businesses...
- 500 Kalamazoo area businesses...
- 18,000 customers...
- 98.5% of customers purchase again...
- Companies like Mega Industries, I.B. Sorry and Bob's Burgers selected us...

- We are a preferred X org vendor...
- 63% of Massachusetts ABC industry companies use us...
- 22,000 installations in 10 states...
- #1 in the tri-state area...
- Do more business than our next 5 competitors combined...
- We typically achieve specific result X...
- One account achieved a 22% increase in _____....
- 3 projects in the last 6 months resulted in a $50,000 or more cost savings...

What do you notice about the above options?

No generalities. Full of specifics.

There are no... we are great, we are swell, we are full-service, superior, we really care for our customers... meaningless generality non-specific garbage. There is none of that.

Write down all possible credibility statements.

Sales script preparation:
Step 4. Writing your benefit statements.

This is the holy grail of writing sales scripts that work.

You must quickly communicate value.

If you communicate value, you can mess up a lot of

things and still win.

Value breaks down doors.

True confession: When I was earning my cold call appointment setting PhD smiling and dialing my way to setting more than 2,000 C-level sales appointments in diverse industries... I used to pretend that the phone line was 3D and I could reach through it and club my decision maker with a 2 x 4. Not kidding.

All you have to work with on the phone is your mouth and your brain.

The 2 x 4 I used were the value and benefit statements conveyed. That is the type of impact you must communicate to have any chance of establishing a foothold in their minds, which leads to a meeting.

Tip: Do not confuse being direct and having impact with ...

... being rude, unprofessional, pushy, too salesy (don't get me going) or the famous "sounding like a telemarketer."

You will never write telephone sales scripts that work by focusing on what you won't do.

Using words with "impact" have nothing to do with coercing or trying to force a result on the phone. Some of the best appointment setters I have ever worked with are soft spoken and speak casually to an extreme, but their words impact like a 2 x 4 and they generate qualified opportunities consistently.

Laser focus on what you must do to craft and deliver sales scripts that work. Think only of those things.

Here are some template benefit statements to get you thinking...

- Decrease cost of X by Y%
- Reduce cycle time by 31%
- Increase revenue by X%
- Increase revenue by X% within 6 months
- Decrease prep time by 1/3
- Competitive advantage
- Eliminate expense
- Eliminate _____
- Reduce X usage by 45%
- Customized solution
- Reliable and consistent
- Single point of contact
- Productivity gains
- Personal productivity
- Cost certainty
- Avoid business interruption
- Less down time
- Faster restore time
- Uniform standards of...

The list could go on and on. To have 30 or more benefit statements in your "pile of words" is not uncommon.

Play "which means what"

Here is a little exercise I recommend to generate impactful ultimate benefits that get the attention of clones of your best accounts.

Play "which means what."

Take your generic vanilla sounding benefit and keep asking "which means what?"

Example: I did a training for a company selling laboratory equipment. They were an industry leader, great reputation, starting to feel the squeeze from lower-cost competition.

One of their benefits was "we thoroughly quality check our products."

Which means what? Our customers don't have to.

Which means what? They save money and increase their margins.

Which means what? Since they can skip the testing step they can roll out new products faster.

Which means what? Faster time to market gives them a competitive advantage over their competition.

Which means what? They get greater market share.

Which means what? Due to our superior testing, when they sell to their customers, there are fewer defects.

Which means what? Customer relationships are weakest when there are performance issues. Since there are fewer performance issues their client retention is higher and that increases profits.

Which means what? And on and on and on.

The point?

A plain vanilla benefit is now related to higher margins, improved time to market, competitive advantage and market share, client retention and ultimately saving the world.

Play "which means what" and see where it leads you. You will think of more ultimate bottom line benefits that matter to your prospects and your competitors are not mentioning. This exercise also helps greatly in fighting price competition by broadening the issues on the table, but that is a totally different topic.

Two super words you should include

Options.
Strategies.

My experience is people want to hear about "options" and "strategies."

Use those words.

What is not on the list

You might have noticed that there is one typical highly touted benefit that is not on the list.

Cost.
Lowest cost.
Inexpensive.
Cheap.
Save money.

Never ever use those words as part of a sales script

benefit. It devalues you. It lumps you in with all the other worthless knuckleheads who can't think of anything substantive to say, so they say, "I can save you money."

Never lead with saving money. It is not what will get you in the door. Doing so attracts the wrong kind of buyers and positions you poorly for a value sale. It is kind of obligatory for you to make reference to costs, but my suggestion is that of the 3 benefits you mention in your script, that references to price, if made at all, be last.

Something like...

"... Companies like A, B, C and 1,500 others selected us as they get monster benefit A, colossal benefit B and competitive pricing..."

At most I recommend you reference "competitive pricing," and mention it last. Contrary to popular belief, pushing low pricing this early in the game will cost you opportunities.

Tip: If people push you on pricing, here are 3 concepts you can use to reply and get the focus off price.

#1. Wear it with pride. "I'll tell you right now, if you are looking for the lowest price and that's all. We are not it."

#2. I would have to be an idiot. "What an incompetent fool I would be, if before I met you, before I was informed about your business objectives, and what has worked and failed in the past for you, before I even knew if what we had would improve your business conditions, I tried to guess at what you need or pricing. Only the desperate or incompetent would do that." (I loved saying that.) Great way to start casting doubt on the credibility of your lower priced competitors.

#3. All I can tell you is. "All I can tell you is that companies like International Amalgamated, Cheapskate Industries and Mega Corp., who check out every possible source on things like this before they commit, looked at all their choices and selected us. Them and about 2,500 others. There are good reasons that they did." Then pause and let that hang in the air.

Then you continue to close on your objective.

There are a few reasons why you want your list of potential benefits to be as extensive as possible.

You sharpen them.
You get to pick the most powerful.
You are more prepared for "first meetings" and more conscious of all the reasons why someone might buy. So you engage in more effective interactions and close more.

All because you are more prepared.

Sales script preparation: Step 5.
What value are you going to deliver at the meeting?

When you seek to obtain a commitment for a meeting, you are selling a value exchange. They meet you in their office, get on the phone with you again, attend a webinar or event. They invest time in order to get something of value.

If that perceived value is worth more than their time, you have a meeting. If that perceived value is worth less than their time, you don't. Simple.

Think of it as a value exchange.

So in order to get their commitment you must communicate a value. But when is that value delivered?

The great unwashed seem to think that the value they communicate assumes that someone hires them, they do a good job and the client is happy. That assumes a lot, is very nebulous and in the minds of that qualified buyer we have on the phone, very unlikely at the time.

So, the value you communicate has to be delivered at the meeting.

At the meeting.

Which approach has the better chance of getting you a meeting?

A. Hi, this is Billy Bob from Mega Industries and we're great, do a super job, really care and want to meet to find out more about your business to see how we can help you. Would next Wednesday at 10 or Thursday at 2:00 be more convenient for you.

B. Hi, this is Billy Bob from Mega Industries. We _____. Companies like A, B, C and 2,000 others work with us as they get enormous benefit 1, gigantic benefit 2 and majestic benefit 3. Would like to introduce ourselves and share specific examples and case histories as to how companies are achieving these results....

Your script has to include a description of what people will get at the meeting if they agree to invest time with you.

It's almost as if you want them thinking, "Well, I probably won't do business with them, but they seem to know what they are doing and I would like to know how other companies get those results. I'll take the meeting."

We know that really is what most of them are thinking.

You don't sell a meeting by saying essentially, "Meet with us because then you will hire us and we will do a good job and get you results down the road and you will be happy." That is way too uncertain, too nebulous and too far in the future to invest time now.

But, if you communicate a value they will get at the meeting that could be helpful to them whether or not they end up working with you...you will sell more meetings.

Sell more meetings, you get more opportunities to sell your product or services to qualified prospects.

So you need to brainstorm all possible descriptions for the value you could deliver at a meeting.

- Examples
- Samples

- Case histories
- Customized analysis
- Proprietary analytics
- A customized report
- A competitive analysis

The more significant and worthwhile the value delivered at the meeting, which they get whether they work with you or not, the more meetings you will get.

For more script tips, samples and updates visit
www.AccordingToScott.com/script-extras

Chapter 7

Completing Your Script Brainstorming

Sales script preparation:
Step 6. Proofs

The next thing you need to do is brainstorm and write down what I call "proofs." Essentially anything you might say which proves or validates what you say should be written down.

- Industry statistics
- Quotes from experts
- Quotes from studies
- Stories from companies you have worked with
- Statements of previous clients
- Reference statements
- Regulatory or government regulations

Anything that proves, illustrates or supports what you say should be written down.

Some of these things will find their way into your sales scripts, responses to objections and gatekeeper interactions. Having them all written down will not only help you to write scripts that set more appointments but you will also be much better prepared to conduct first meetings that sell a constructive next step.

The better your proofs the more meetings you set and the more you will close.

Sales script preparation:
Step 7. Ear Candy.

Last but not least in your "pile of words" are what I call "ear candy."

When I am working with a company or salesperson on scripting I read a ton of stuff. Marketing materials, industry reports, articles. Look at competitors' websites and review other sources. Many times there are words or phrases that jump out at me. They are memorable, grabbers. They sound great and can make my scripts come alive.

Anything that jumps out at you or is particularly intriguing, write it all down. If it doesn't fit neatly into any of the above categories, stick it in your "ear candy" section.

When I do this for a project I typically have at least 2 pages single spaced with ear candy stuff. It is the reservoir you draw from. Make it as deep as possible.

Sales script preparation:
Step 8. Write down all objections and repetitive
scenarios you anticipate hearing.

Once you write your core scripts, you will turn
your attention to writing responses to resistance and
common scenarios.

When you hear certain questions, objections and
statements over and over again, it is reasonable for you
to anticipate them and have already thought about the
best thing to say.

You hear something for the umpteenth time. Click.
Whirr. Boom. You respond completely, confidently and
with the words most calculated to attain your business
result. You are prepared.

When I give trainings, it is pretty easy to pick out
the top producing successful salespeople from the
wannabe's who never will be, and those working way
too hard for too few results.

When asked what they say when they hear "X" from a
prospect, the top producers give a complete confident
response. You think, "Hey, they have actually thought
about this."

But the wannabe's? Ask them the same question as to
an objection or question they have heard 100 times and
you get...,"Ummmm, Ahhhhhh, well, no two situations
are exactly alike, you never know, it depends. Um.
Ah." Inexcusable.

The reason many people are working hard at sales
and not earning to their capabilities is simply that they

don't approach sales as a craft. They let numerous opportunities go by to get better and improve their skills.

If you are going to get great results prospecting on the phone you have to identify common scenarios, responses, objections and questions. Write them all down.

Once you have created your "piles of words" and initial core scripts, you can then turn your attention to crafting verbiage with the best chance of accomplishing your business objectives whenever you come across a repetitive scenario.

> You hear it.
> You have anticipated it.
> You thought about the best response.
> You wrote it down.
> You rewrote, massaged and improved it.
> You are prepared.
> You deliver the words confidently and smoothly.
> You accomplish your business objective.

Write down all repetitive scenarios you come across.

Where do you get all this stuff?

Easy.

- Interview callers and salespeople from your company or industry.

- Scour your company website.

- Review the websites of your competitors.

- Note those that sell what you offer online. Their verbiage has to be very sharp and impactful. Take notes.

- Pretend that you are a buyer. Surf online. Go to the places buyers might go and take notes on verbiage.

- Review marketing materials of your company and competitors.

- Look at RFP's.

- Find and read relevant articles.

Creating your "pile of words" just takes some time, patience and thinking. Skip this step at your certain peril. If you are thinking that you don't have time to adequately prepare, then you are doomed. Just face that fact right now.

You have your piles of words. Now what? Write your scripts.

My hesitation in writing this book was that the many who deliriously think a "good script" will solve all their sales problems, will think this is all they need. Wrong.

Good scripts won't help you if you are not talking to the right people. They won't help you if you are not talking to enough of them.

Those factors are determined by your overall setup and what I call your prospecting infrastructure. Whom are you calling. The contact manager/crm you are using. How it is setup. Your call process. Much more.

Those factors determine the efficiency of your calling and how many conversations you have with top decision makers at qualified targets.

Your scripts determine your effectiveness at converting those conversations into the result you seek. Face to face meetings, phone meetings, webinars or attendance at events. Those results are all obtained with the same structures and script building processes.

"Good scripts" won't save you if your total prospecting system is not in place. Let's assume that has been done and done well.

Scripts are necessary

Why is it necessary for you to work from a script? Because you have very little time and every second counts, and if you do not plan out ahead of time the words you will say to get the results you seek, you are going to dilute your effectiveness.

If it takes you 40 seconds to say things you could say in 30 seconds you will lose opportunities. If your decision maker tunes you out because your opening is not good or you haven't given them a reason to listen in the first 3 seconds, you will lose opportunities. If you don't convey all the things that are necessary for you to convey for "qualified buyers" to agree to talk to you a bit more or decide to go to the next step with you, you will lose opportunities.

On the phone everything is compressed by a factor of about 10. If you are face to face with someone they might indulge you a few minutes of small talk before they expect you to get to the point. Or, they conclude that you are wasting their time and discount you totally. But on the phone that takes only seconds.

At a face to face meeting they might give you 30 or 40 minutes of attention to state your case, but on the phone you only get a few moments to state your case and reach your objective. So, if you are not prepared, meaning that you have planned in advance how to make maximum use of every precious second you have to state your case and get where you want to go, you will lose opportunities.

For more script tips, samples and updates visit
www.AccordingToScott.com/script-extras

Chapter 8

Focus on Buyers Only.
Forget everyone else.

Now let me also say something else very bluntly. When planning out what you have to say to reach your objectives, you have to focus on connecting with those people who have a need that you can fill, and totally disregard everyone else. Let me say that again. Focus only on those who have a need you can fill, totally, I mean totally disregard everyone else.

Focus on those that not only have a need you can fill, and whom, if they heard the right things, would agree to a substantive "first step" with you. Following that, they would participate in a sales process that leads to a purchase on acceptable terms. Buyers.

Focus solely on "buyers." Throw the rest down the stairs.

The reality is, that most of the people we choose to prospect, most of the people we will have a conversation with, do not have a need that we can fill. They are going to say "no," Not at this time, take me off your list. That's fine. In fact, getting a solid "yes" or a solid "no," is a perfectly acceptable response. The faster you can get a clear "yes" or "no," the better you will be at prospecting.

Phone success today requires unrelenting focus on the needs, wants and hot buttons of those who are going to buy. Any weakening or watering down of your verbiage at all costs you qualified prospects, meetings and closed sales.

You don't want to annoy people?
Worry more about connecting with buyers.

Understand something. No matter what you say or how you say it, you are going to speak to people who don't need what you offer. Some people, once they realize you can't help them, will be bothered by the interruption. Others will be naturally grumpy or having a bad day.

There is nothing you can do about any of those things.

Whether people are bothered or annoyed by your call has much more to do with them and their circumstances than it has to do with you.

Many, with the goal of "not wanting to annoy people," water down what they say and ease into a call with ridiculous questions like, "How are you?" or "Do you have a minute?"

It has always fascinated me that those who try their hardest to "not annoy" people, are in fact the ones who annoy the most.

When you are clear and concise and state very directly what you do, your credibility, benefits and what you want, professional people respect that and act accordingly. In all my years of calling, and remember I set more than 2,000 C-Level appointments, I could count on 1 hand the number that were rude or hung up.

Maybe's are death

Remember, the "maybe's" are what will kill your prospecting efforts. So all your script paths must be engineered to obtain a very clear "yes" or "no."

Stop worrying about the vast majority of people you will contact who don't have a need. Worry only about communicating effectively with those prospects that do have a need.

If a "buyer" picks up the phone and says "hello," do you say the things that enable buyers to conclude that you are worth listening to a bit longer.

In my calling days (Remember, I set more than 2,000 C-level sales appointments in very diverse industries) my fear was always that a buyer, someone that had a need my client could fill and was going to eventually write a big check to somebody, would say "Hello" and I didn't say the words that enabled them to conclude that I was worth listening to a bit longer. First a few seconds longer, then a few minutes, then at a meeting, phone conference, webinar or event.

Do not spend even 2 seconds being concerned with the non-buyers. My attitude and belief is that if someone does not have a need, they can state that after they know what you do, why you are credible, the benefits you deliver and the value they get if they meet with you. That takes 30 seconds.

Make them choke

Make the buyers choke on the words, "We're all set" because you are saying words that communicate value meaningful to them and they are listening.

They say that those who are best at finding gold, are best at determining what is not gold. And that is also true in prospecting for sales. The faster you can work through a group of prospects and determine who does not have a need you can fill, the faster you will uncover those who do have a need you can fill.

Many think this is a game of qualification. They are wrong. Sales prospecting and appointment setting is a game of disqualification. The faster you can disqualify someone, the fewer calls and resources are directed to them. That time, calling and money can now be spent on qualified prospects.

It is counter-intuitive but you are not trying to keep leads alive... you are trying to kill them.

Please follow me with this rant as it goes to the core of the script structure strategy that I have seen work so well and recommend to you.

Most of those who seek to set appointments are selling something that is not purchased at short intervals.

The types of purchases that can economically justify a calling effort are typically made every few years or longer. If it is a service relationship, again, it's a vendor relationship that is not changed lightly. It may only come up for reassessment every few years.

What percentage of your target group is in play?

So the bottom line is, even in a very qualified group of suspects, only a certain percentage of that group is in play. Meaning, they have a recognized need and if they heard the right things and felt comfortable they would buy.

There is always a certain percentage of the market that is buying from someone, right now. People and companies are writing checks to competitors. There is no reason they shouldn't be writing them to you. All you have to do is connect the dots.

My assumption and judgment is that about 1/6 of any qualified group being called is in play. The rest are not.

So the game is not to try to convince anyone of anything. Let me say that again. Your "set the appointment" scripts do not seek to convince anyone of anything." You are not trying to convince anyone they have a problem worth solving.

What you are doing with your scripts is to enable those that already recognize they have a need that you are worth spending more time with. That's all.

When you bump into a buyer, you are direct, clear and concise about what you do, your credibility, the benefits clients get from you and the value you will deliver to them. BOOM!

Focus only on that. Stating the words that enable buyers to grasp that you can help them.

Don't water down what you say

The non-buyers? Don't even spend 2 seconds thinking about them. Think only of what will enable buyers to go to the next step. Many make the mistake of watering down what they say to have more comfortable conversations with those who will never buy. The problem with that is when you bump into a buyer on the phone, your words are less clear, less impactful, you are not communicating your credibility and benefits quick enough or effectively. Buyers don't "get it," so they say goodbye.

You did all the work. You got a buyer on the phone. They didn't get your value or grasp that you were worth spending time with. Call ends without a next step. Why? Because you were thinking more about non-buyers. You did the work. You got a buyer on the phone. You hung up with nothing.

You should be deathly afraid of getting a buyer on the phone and not saying the words that enable them to understand you can help them and are worth spending more time with.

So, to communicate your worth and to avoid watering down what you say, you must work from a script.

Script writing

You will need 4 core scripts to start with. Get these

right first. All of your scripts will flow easily once you get these core scripts right.

You will need an "identify the decision maker" script, a "set the meeting" script, a "voicemail" script and a group of "response to resistance" scripts. In order to achieve the purpose intended, those scripts have to be structured in a certain way.

For more script tips, samples and updates visit
www.AccordingToScott.com/script-extras

Chapter 9

Your "Identify the Decision-Maker" Script.

Let's take the first script, the "identify the decision maker" script. You have a list of companies you have decided to prospect, and you either don't know who the decision maker is, or you have a name that you think is the decision maker and you have to confirm it.

Now let's set the scene up. You are calling into Mega Corporation and you are probably going to get the main receptionist, who is handling too many incoming calls and some administrative chores.

Your objective on this first call is to identify the decision maker only. As a bonus you may be able to get the direct dial or extension number and some "potential worth" information. Your objective is not to talk to them, your objective is to get the information you need to move forward on that account.

Let's assume that you don't have a name and you are gunning for the person who makes marketing and advertising decisions. There are other titles you might contact, but let's use the marketing director as an example.

Overwhelmed receptionist picks up the phone and says, "Thank you for calling Mega Corp, how can I help you?"

You say, "I was looking to send some information to whoever handles your marketing and advertising. Can you tell me who to direct it to?"

Or a slight variation of that would be, " I was looking to send some information to whoever handles the purchase of your computers or technology equipment. Can you tell me who to direct it to?"

Or, another variation of the identify the decision maker script would be, " Hi, I was looking to send some information to your vice president of sales. Could you tell me who to direct it to?"

Now let's think about this for a moment. Most salespeople call companies to speak to decision makers and it is the receptionist's job to protect them from harassment. All you are indicating is that you want to send them some information.

Now what do you think overwhelmed receptionist is thinking? All this person wants to do is send some information, information that is going to be thrown away anyway. Sure, no problem. And because you are very much not acting like an aggressive or typical salesperson, but are acting very nonchalant, almost uncaring about the answer, 19 times out of 20, you will get the name with the first call.

If you don't have a name, the script is, "I was looking to send some information to your MIS director. Could you tell me who to send it to?"

Let there be no doubt as to what you want

That script is very direct and tells the receptionist exactly what it is that you want. There is no doubt whatsoever as to what you want, so they can give you the answer. 19 times out of 20 they will say... send it to Cindy Server.

Notice anything interesting about this "identify the decision maker" script? Did I identify myself or the company I am calling from? No I did not. Why?

Is your name necessary at this step

Well, there are really 3 reasons I don't identify myself on an "Identify the decision maker" call.

First, I have found that I can get the same result without identifying myself as when I do identify myself. Frankly, making these calls probably isn't the favorite thing you do in this world so every word you can cut out and every second of boredom and tedium you can eliminate from your life, the better.

Second, receptionists and gatekeepers have their antennae up for anyone who is going to make them look bad or harass their superiors. The more information you give them, the less information they have to possibly conclude that you are one of them. In fact, you should make this call with the most bored, nonchalant non-caring attitude you can muster... the bored part should be no problem.

Third, most people, particularly people new to sales, when you identify yourself and your company to a receptionist, immediately red flag yourself as the exact type of person they don't want to cooperate with.... "Hi, this is Scott Channell from Mega Industries, how are you today? That's great. Weather treating you right down there is it? That's great. How about those Red Sox? Say, I was looking to send some information to whoever is in charge of sales. Could you tell me who to send it to?"

Pleasssseeeee. Click. Don't red flag yourself. Be simple. Be direct. Be nonchalant. Get your info. Hang up. Click.

3 bits of info you need to get

Once you get the name there are 3 other bits of information you should try to obtain.

1. Worth information.
2. Direct dial or extension number.
3. Email address and/or fax number.

A little explanation... remember I said a while ago that appointment setting was more a process of active disqualification. We try to find reasons to stop calling people. Yes, along the way you will also identify those worth more of your time, but you need script strategies that enable you to identify the non-qualified and reallocate time that would be spent chasing them to either higher worth suspects or a pool of suspects that contain higher worth suspects.

That process starts here. So, after they say, "Send it to Cindy Server," you say, "Great, just so I know what to send do you happen to know X?

"X" being something that gives you some insight into whether they might be a high, medium or low potential worth suspect.

"... Just so I know what to send, do you happen to know..."

... How many employees are in the company?
... How many salespeople you have?
... How many employee moves you do a year?
... Whether payroll is done weekly or bi-weekly?

Ask a question that gives you some insight into the potential worth of the suspect so that you can properly allocate your time.

You get the answer and continue..

"... When I follow up, is there a direct dial or extension number to use?"

And if you are feeling really lucky...

"Thanks, would you have an email address or fax number to send this to?

Boom. Boom. Boom. Boom.

> Name.
> Worth info.
> Direct dial or extension number.
> Email address or fax number.

Now, are you going to be able to ask all those questions? You will not. But with every gatekeeper interaction, with every call that does not result in a conversation with your decision maker you should be trying to increase the quality of the information you are working with. Your script paths help you to allocate time and resources for maximum results.

It is very important to attempt to get some type of qualifying information on every call. The reality is that most dials you make are not going to connect with your target. That doesn't mean it is a wasted call. You can still improve the quality of your calls, and direct more of your time toward higher return targets if you can improve the quality of the information you are working with.

In the above example, the qualifying question might be, "Oh, just so I know what to send, about how many employees are there in your company?" If a company with 1,000 or more employees is a much better prospect than a company with 100 employees, you can get that information and allocate your time accordingly. As you identify more and more companies that fit your high priority target profile, you can allocate more calling time to them.

Other examples. When I started out, I used to do a lot of work in the employee relocation industry, for companies that moved top corporate executives all over the world. Obviously, a company doing 250 moves or more a year was a much better potential target than a company doing 25 moves a year. In sales training the question is, "just so I know what to send, approximately how many salespeople are there in the company?" You get the answer and invest your time accordingly.

What questions would help you?

The Direct Dial or Extension number.

In order for your scripts to get you appointments, you have to have conversations with top decision makers. You greatly increase the odds of having more conversations with top decision makers when you get good at collecting direct dial and extension numbers.

How do you get the direct dial or extension number? You ask for it. Every chance you get. Anytime you interact with somebody other than the decision makers, you ask for the direct dial or extension number.

The more direct dial and extension numbers you stockpile the more conversations you will have. More conversations, more opportunity for your great scripts to get you appointments.

Email addresses and fax numbers

This is a primer about scripts, not all the elements of an effective call process. But suffice it to say that your script paths can enable you to work the most effective overall call process. What starts with a cold call ends up being something quite different because you should be "touching" your target parallel to your dial attempts.

Allow me a slight detour. There is a basic rule of marketing 101 that says people have to be touched by us about 7 times before they can absorb and grasp our message and take action. When I started out calling pre-internet, the touch options were voicemail, fax and snail mail.

Warning: Contrary to rumor and wishful thinking, sending mail to "warm up a call" is a total and complete waste of money. People like to cling to the illusion that a postcard or mail missive somehow has top decision makers marveling at your prose and staring at the phone awaiting your call. Rather than make a "cold call" you are now making a "warm call." If you believe that you probably suffer from other delusions.

The exact opposite is true. When you dial, dial, dial, dial and dial and finally get a top dog to pick up and say "hello," when you start with, "Hi, this is Charlie Chatty from I. B. Sorry just following up on a letter sent about..... "

Bye bye commission check. 99% of the time you hear "Didn't get it. Didn't read it. Send it again." Now, by your own choice of words, after all your hard work, when you have a high worth top decision maker with a need you can fill who would love to meet with a highly credible vendor that delivers benefits they want and would meet to get the value you would deliver at a meeting... by your own choice and self-sabotaging actions you are jibber jabbering about something that relates nothing about what you do, why you are so credible, the benefits people get from working with you and the value they would get at a meeting.

You have impaled yourself.

But I digress. The point of this is that your call process should incorporate a series of "touches." This is so that your target gets a consistent impactful message. You increase the chance that a qualified target absorbs your message and acts upon it.

They might call you. Email you. Fax you. Mail a request to you. When you do get them on the phone they may be a bit familiar with your talking points and more likely to agree to meet.

Your script paths support that effort by providing the email addresses and fax numbers for your touch system.

Two points.

1. When I started out fax was prevalent. Now, when you mention faxing, people start chuckling: Equating it with the pony express or blast faxing. Both ideas are wrong. A fax is just a touch. A fax that works is far removed from what a blast fax looks like and is delivered as part of a much different process. Few today use fax as part of their appointment setting process. Of those who do, many report great success. You can bump results 10% - 20% with very little extra effort and cost if incorporated into your process correctly. Don't be super quick to dismiss it. It's just a touch.

2. Mail. Using mail to bump response to an appointment setting campaign is a bad idea. Can't

think of even one example of it working and I have been doing this 18 years. Mail can be a great lead generation and marketing tool. But the marketing math has to work totally independently of any impact on appointment setting.

For more script tips, samples and updates visit
www.AccordingToScott.com/script-extras

Chapter 10

Your "Set the Meeting" Script.

This is the situation. After making a lot of initial calls to identify a decision maker, and then a lot of follow up calls to get them to pick up the phone, a decision maker you are targeting picks up the phone. Your objective is to obtain an agreement to meet with you. Let me give you two variations of a set the meeting script.

Set the meeting script number 1: Your target picks up the phone.

"Hello."

"This is Pauline prospector from Super Service Group. We specialize in providing widgets, wadgets, hardware, design, and implementation services. Companies like Mega Corp, Brito Corporation and International

Amalgamated work with us due to our expertise, quick response and competitive pricing. If you are looking for information or options regarding your widgets, wadgets or equipment supplier, we would like to introduce ourselves, and provide information on a few things we do different that have proven valuable. Would you have any time in the next week or 2?"

Now it is typical to work through a number of scripts before you settle upon the one that feels most comfortable and gets the results you want.

Here is set the meeting script number 2: Your target picks up the phone.

"Hello."

"This is Paul Prospector from Super Service Group. We specialize in helping companies select widgets, wadgets and gizmos which best meet their needs. Companies like L. L. Bean, Lycos and Dow Jones use us because we are experts and our prices are very competitive. I have no idea if you might be looking for information or options regarding technology equipment. If you are, we would like the opportunity to introduce ourselves, give you some information and strategies to improve delivery time and reduce costs. If you hear something you like and think of us in the future that would be great. Would you have any time in the next week or 2?"

The format of these scripts works. Any sale is only as strong as the foundation it is built upon. This script structure is the foundation.

Understand that in order to achieve your intended

result, there are impressions you must be prepared to convey. If you do not convey them you have no right to realistically think your target is going to agree to a meeting. The less you convey, the less successful you will be. Not only do you have to convey certain impressions, but you have to do it within the parameters of two rules for successful first conversations.

You have 3 seconds to click

Within the first 3 seconds after saying hello, your target is going to make a decision. Is this person worth listening to or not. Is this person someone who is wasting my time or someone who may have something that is beneficial to me. Within the first 3 seconds of your target saying "hello," you must plant in their minds the impression that it would be beneficial to them, to listen to you a bit longer.

If they do not have that mindset, then assuming that you are speaking to someone who has a need that you can fill and would be willing to act, it really doesn't matter what you say after that, because their mind has shut down. They have made an initial judgment that you are not worthwhile.

I really do believe that once their mind shuts down, that you could tell them that you want to show up to their office with $1,000 cash as a gift with no strings attached and they would turn you down. They don't perceive you as someone who is worthwhile so nothing you say has any impact on them.

Notice also that I phrased what you had to do in the first 3 seconds based upon the assumption that you

were talking to someone who had a need you could fill
and would be willing to act.

Those are the people you are seeking to influence. You
must give those people the information they need to
conclude that they should talk with you, meet with you,
and explore a proposal with you.

If they do not have a need you can fill or they would
not be willing to act, then what they think about you
is irrelevant. Think about making an initial connection
with those who have a need you can fill within seconds
of getting them to pick up the phone.

Let's dissect a script.

Let's use the second meeting script as an example.

The opening is, "My name is Pauline prospector
from Super Service Group. We specialize in helping
companies select widgets, wadgets and gizmos which
best meet their needs. Companies like L. L. Bean,
Lycos and Dow Jones use us because we are experts
and our prices are very competitive."

What have we done within seconds of getting our
decision maker on the phone? We have identified
who we are and where we are calling from, we have
told them clearly and very directly what it is we do.
We specialize in helping companies select widgets,
wadgets and gizmos that best meet their needs.

We have absolutely slayed them with a credibility
statement that communicates we are not small time, we
are not fly by nights, we are not small players.

We have delivered a statement that communicates

credibility unquestionably. When you drop names like L. L. Bean, Lycos and Dow Jones you instantly communicate that you are a player, that you are knowledgeable and that you are credible.

Now, if you have connected with someone who has a need for widgets, wadgets and gizmos, you have told them within seconds that this is what you do. They don't have to guess or speculate about what you do while they listen to the rest of your spiel.

You have communicated unquestionably that you are a substantial player in this industry because you dropped 3 names of companies that would not do business with less than a top shelf player.

So within seconds of hello, *if that person on the other end of the line has a need,* let me say again, *if that person on the other end of the line has a need,* you have given them CAUSE FOR PAUSE. You have planted the thought in their head, "Hey maybe I should listen a bit longer. I have those specs on my desk now, or that order coming up in a few months. My current vendor is a bit shaky, I am not really happy with the level of service I am getting, they do what I need done, and they help companies select widgets, wadgets and gizmos. They must know what they are doing or they wouldn't have clients like L. L. Bean, Lycos, and Dow Jones. I will listen a bit longer because there might be something in it for me. They might make my job easier, do a better job than my current vendors, save me some money."

That is what you need to happen within seconds of connecting with someone who has a need that you can fill.

Now a couple of observations here. First of all, understand that people think 10 times faster than they can speak or listen. So in addition to people listening to what you say, there is an avalanche of thoughts going through their heads and you want them to be positive. You can't give them time to think on their own, because the natural gravity of the situation is for them to mentally conclude that you are an idiot, that you don't have what they need, that you are bothering them and that you seem nice but have nothing of value. They want to get you off the phone as soon as possible so they can get back to what they are doing.

Notice what I did not recommend that you do in these first few seconds. And I know that these next few comments are going to rub a few people the wrong way. They always do.

Things nobody cares about

Notice that I did not say, "Hi, how are you today? This is Pauline Perky or Charlie Chatty from Super Service group and I was wondering if you have a few moments? Is this a good time to talk?

First of all, nobody cares. You don't care about how they are doing, and they know you don't care about how they are doing today, so such drivel wastes precious seconds.

It also gives them time to conclude that you are like all the other "teleprospectors" who waste their time.

Don't make it easy for them
to lump you in with the idiots

If you say the things that idiots say, they will conclude that you are also an idiot wishing to waste their time.

Why shouldn't they conclude that? They get a lot of calls. Most of them are from amateurs. The vast majority of them are a bother and a waste of their time.

So what have you done with your, "Hi, how are you, is this a good time, do you have a few minutes" banter in the first precious seconds of your conversation?"

You have given them the time to conclude they should get rid of you. *You have given them no reasons to conclude that it may be in their best interests to listen to you a bit further.*

Now part of my strong feeling on this is experience, I know many people feel more comfortable with the social chit-chat on the first contact. I have never seen it work on the initial phone call when someone is trying to create a successful prospecting program. I personally would feel more comfortable if it did.

My personal preference would be that I have a comfortable relaxed conversation with a prospect on the phone. I personally wish that the, "Hi, how are you, is this a bad time, have you got a few minutes?" type of banter would work. If it did I would use it. But it doesn't.

If it works for you, and if you are able to generate all the new accounts you need and hit your numbers and produce to your full potential with that type of opening line to a total stranger on the phone, I would say that is great. Great for you. But I do not want to be wishy-washy on this at all. I have not seen it work that way.

Let's look at it another way. The people you are targeting are top executives making fairly large economic decisions that have far more impact than just the price of what they are purchasing. They are busy. I would assume that they are busy, I would assume that the kind of person who is going to buy enough product or services to make you a lot of money is a busy person.

So why give them the opportunity to say they are busy and terminate the call before I can tell them what I can do and just how credible we are. Much of the work I have done has been for companies that are making major sales. People who make those types of decisions are busy.

This is the real world; the people we are trying to communicate with are difficult to reach. They don't know us. They don't know what we do and don't know just how good we are until we tell them. Until that information is provided these busy decision makers have no basis to conclude that we are worth their time, that we are better than anyone else, that we are credible, that we can help them. They don't know until we tell them.

You are interrupting them. Get over it.

Also, let's also be very direct about something. You are interrupting them. If someone has no need that we can fill, is perfectly happy with their supplier, they can say, "I am not interested and have no time for this," after they know what we can do and how credible we are.

But the people who have no need we can fill are not

my concern. I don't care about them. I care only about connecting with the decision makers who have a need that we can fill, and communicating the information they need to conclude that maybe they should listen to me a bit longer. If I don't give them that information, they cannot make that conclusion.

We have to interrupt their train of thought and pull them away from whatever else they are doing when they picked up the phone. So it is an interruption to launch immediately into your spiel when they pick up the phone, but I believe fervently that you have no choice. There are certain things you have to communicate within seconds, or you will lose those whom do have a need you can fill, because you have given them no information upon which they conclude you are worth more of their time. Enough said.

So we start out. Your prospect says, "hello." and our script begins "This is Charlie Chatty from Super Service Group. We specialize in helping companies select widgets, wadgets and gizmos that best meet their needs. Companies like L.L. Bean, Lycos and Dow Jones use us because we are experts and our prices are very competitive."

Now we continue with the rest of the script, and here my personal preference is to change the pace and tone of the script. So where in the first few seconds I am very direct and straightforward, now as I get into second number 10 or so, I adopt a different tone.

The script would continue like this. "I have no idea if you might be looking for information or options regarding technology equipment. If you are, we would like the opportunity to introduce ourselves to you, give you some information and strategies companies have used to reduce delivery times and cut costs. If you hear something you like and think of us in the future that would be great. Would you have any time in the next week or two?

 Boom . End of script. Now you do the hardest thing in the world for a salesperson to do. You shut up and listen.

Let's dissect the rest of the script.

 "I have no idea if you might be looking for information or options regarding your technology equipment."

 With that sentence we have changed the tone to be a bit more laid back, and notice that the language is very open ended. We don't know anything about the needs of who we are calling so we use very broad general terms like "information" or "options" or "strategies." I have discovered that people love "strategies" so try to work that into your scripts whenever you can.

 So what we have done with the middle of the script is change the tone a bit and admit the obvious. "We have no idea whether they are looking"... we have phrased things in a very general way ... information or options... That doesn't eliminate much ... regarding your technology equipment. Which clarifies what we do so that there is no confusion.

 That is a lot for one sentence to do but that structure does it well. In about 18 seconds we have stated who we are, where we are calling from, what we do and why we are so credible. We have oriented their thinking to where we need it to be. Are they looking for information or options regarding the purchase of technology equipment?

Now with our last statement, tell them specifically, clearly and unequivocally, exactly what it is we want them to do. So we end up,... "If you are, we would like the opportunity to introduce ourselves and give you some information on some programs that other companies have found valuable. If you hear something you like and think of us in the future that would be great. Would you have any time in the next week or two?"

Boom! End of script.

We are accomplishing a number of things with that last line. We are asking for the opportunity to introduce ourselves. That goes down a lot easier and is a lot softer than saying, " We want to meet with you to try to sell you something." That statement does not create any resistance from our target.

"We want to give you some information on things we do differently and some programs that other companies have found valuable." What have we conveyed?

We are going to give them information on things that other companies have found valuable. Maybe we have something they could benefit from. Other companies have benefited, maybe we will.

The sentence continues ..."If you hear something you like and think of us in the future that would be great. Would you have any time in the next week or two?" What we do with that statement is take away all the pressure and deflate resistance to a meeting. We talk about introducing ourselves and giving them information on valuable programs. We tell them that if they think of us in the future, that would be great.

We are communicating to them that we are not going to push them to sign a purchase order at this meeting, we are not going to pressure them, and then we tell them clearly and very directly what it is we need to know. Do they have any time in the next week or 2?

For more script tips, samples and updates visit
www.AccordingToScott.com/script-extras

Chapter 11

Your "Voice Mail" Script.

Very few people who listen to a voicemail will return the call. (How insightful!) Although some will and that is what we want to happen, the purpose is also to act as a commercial, which works in conjunction with your other touches to increase name recognition and increase their recognition of exactly what it is that Super Service Group does.

Consistency of messaging builds credibility and recognition.

Very simply, voicemail is a touch and the more touches we deliver to a prospect with a concise direct consistent message; the more likely it is that they will recognize who we are and what we might do for them. If that happens, it increases the chance they will respond to a touch, call you if they have a need, or be more receptive to your phone call. That is why we leave voicemail messages. It is part of a total strategy to penetrate the minds of our prospects.

Here is the script. "If you are looking to replace widgets, wadgets or gizmos, companies like L. L. Bean, Lycos and Dow Jones use us to select and install systems that best meet their needs. If you are looking for information or a quote, we can help. This is Charlie Chatty from Super Service Group 1-800-123-45xx extension 1234."

This is a 20-second script. Look at all that you do in 20 seconds. "If you are looking to replace widgets, wadgets or gizmos" Boom, in the first 3 seconds of your message you have just told them simply and directly what it is you do. If they have a need, they will hopefully listen for a few more seconds before deleting you.

Picture this. Top decision makers listen to their voice mails with their finger hovering over the delete button. The task of your voice mail script is to keep it hovering.

Then you continue, "Companies like L. L. Bean, Lycos and Dow Jones selected us..." Look at what has happened here within 6 seconds, *if someone who has a need you can fill* is listening, they know without doubt what you do and that that you might be able to help them. Not only that, you have slayed them by dropping three recognizable names communicating that you are a player and someone with credibility in the industry.

Now, if they have a need you can fill, they know that,

and they know you are credible, all within 7 seconds. Now you continue... "L.L. Bean, Lycos and Dow Jones use us to select and install systems that best meet their needs. If you are looking for information or a quote, we can help. This is Charlie Chatty from Super Service group, 800-123-4567 extension 1234."

When we finish up we ask a broad question... "If you are looking for information or a quote, we can help." Now finally at the end we tell them who we are, from where and our phone number.

What is weird about this script? You don't identify yourself or leave your number until the very end.

Why? Let's think about it. If someone who has a need we can fill is listening to us, the probability is that as soon as we identify ourselves as a teleprospector, given that most teleprospectors waste the time of decision makers, we get deleted. That finger stops hovering and hits delete.

But if we structure the script as related, within the first 3 seconds we have their attention and within the first 7 seconds we have conveyed credibility, so if they have a need we can fill, we have a real shot of them at least listening to the message.

Now of course if they are not a person who has a need we can fill, they will also know that within seconds and will delete you. So what.

For more script tips, samples and updates visit
www.AccordingToScott.com/script-extras

Chapter 12

Scripts to Respond to Objections

Let's now focus on a common obstacle to getting face to face with a well qualified high worth prospect. Responding to objections.

You have done a great job at organizing yourself for prospecting success. Your "identify the decision maker" scripts have served up names, direct dial and extension numbers, worth information and maybe even email addresses and fax numbers of many quality targets. You have everything coded, your "set the appointment" scripts are written and rehearsed and you just love to smile and dial. You consistently implement your call process, which includes a planned sequence of calls and touches calculated to get a prospect to pick up the phone and get the opportunity to deliver your pitch.

Let's not discount the effort that it takes to get a target to pick up the phone. You have to make preliminary calls to identify or confirm the identity of your decision maker. Then you are going to call, call, call to get them to pick up the phone. It's a lot of effort to get someone to pick up the phone.

This means that when a target does pick up the phone, you obviously want to maximize the chance that that conversation will turn into a face to face meeting. The best way to get a new account by far is to schedule an appointment with the prospect.

How many "first meetings" do you need?

My experience is that it takes 4 - 7 initial "first meeting" appointments set with new prospects to gain a new account. If your close rate with people you meet cold is much more than 7 or 8 to 1, then my opinion is that you need to look at your process. Either the pool you are calling is the wrong pool for some reason, or you need to adjust your sales process. Look at what you do at a first meeting, how you follow up, how you make proposals, how you close. Even great salespeople rarely have much better than a 3 or 4 to 1 ratio of new first appointments to a new account closed ratio.

When you invest substantial time in prospecting, you want to set as many appointments as possible because there is a reasonable relationship between the number of appointments you set and the number of new accounts you bring in.

If you are like many salespeople, very busy handling your existing accounts and finding it a challenge to fit prospecting into your routine, it is important that you get 1 hour's worth of value for every hour you spend prospecting. It is very easy to get only 15 minutes of value or only 30 minutes worth of value from every hour invested in prospecting if you are inefficient or ineffective.

If you are not generating conversations, then this advice on objections will do you little good. If you are not generating conversations, my best advice would be to take a good hard realistic look at how you are organizing yourself and processing the records you have selected to prospect.

If you find that a good number of companies you call are too small and that in order to make some phone calls you have to wade through a lot of records, If too many names on your database no longer work there, or are non-decision makers, then you are working very inefficiently, will have a very low number of conversations per hour invested in prospecting, and of course not have many sales appointments to show for your efforts.

If you feel you are in that situation and want to change it, ask for help. The biggest thing you can do to turn that situation around is to keep a weekly score sheet that tracks how many new target prospects you dump into your funnel every week, how many conversations you have and how many meetings you book.

If you keep those records, you can constantly make marginal improvements in how many new companies you call, how many conversations you have per hour and what your conversion rate of conversations to meetings is.

But let's assume that you are prospecting efficiently and are now determined to improve upon your conversation to booked meeting ratio. You must understand and appreciate six concepts to effectively respond to objections.

1. You are fighting gravity.

The normal natural knee jerk most common reaction a decision maker has to a teleprospector's request to schedule a meeting is forgetaboutit. Why?

They don't have time, they have no need, they have had too much time wasted by teleprospector's that called before you, so they say "no." Your targets' immediate thought when they realize they are being prospected, is to think, "I am not going to do this."

For you to achieve the purpose of your call you have to reverse gravity. In order to break free from gravity you must project a force more powerful than gravity. What you say and how you say it must contain enough energy to overcome a decision maker's normal natural reaction not to schedule a meeting with you. You will only do that if you take calculated actions, are prepared, and practice.

2. You don't really hear "objections."

When prospecting we want to effectively overcome objections. But let me ask you this question. Do you think it is really accurate to think of what we seek to overcome as "objections." Let me explain. I think that for something to be accurately labeled an "objection" it has to be based upon some knowledge, some level of familiarity, some modicum of understanding, and appreciation of what is being presented so that someone can truly and meaningfully "object" to it.

Is that really what is happening when we are prospecting? It might be more appropriate to entitle this section "overcoming resistance." It is normal and natural for our targets to resist our efforts to schedule a meeting with them. They resist our efforts by speaking words that sound very similar to someone who is raising an "objection." Although the words sound the same they are substantively different, and because they are substantively different, your response to them has to be different in order to achieve the purpose of your phone call.

But when we are prospecting, our objective is not to sell our products or services. We are trying to sell a meeting, not to close a deal. When we are prospecting, we are not overcoming objections as much as we are responding to resistance, and when seeking to schedule a sales appointment, when responding to resistance, what we purposely leave unsaid, is just as important to achieving our objective, as what we choose to say.

At the closing stage of the sales process, if we don't fully satisfy the prospect and give them all the information they request, the deal does not get closed. But when prospecting, if we fully satisfy the prospect, answer all their questions and give them all the information they request, there is no longer a reason for them to meet with us. We have knocked ourselves out of the "set the sales appointment" game.

3. People don't meet with you because you don't give them enough reason to meet with you.

Remember that the number 1 reason prospects don't agree to meet with you is because you don't give them enough reason to meet ... and the reasons prospects should meet with you have to be delivered at the first meeting.

So when you engage your prospect in a conversation, you have to always keep in mind, that in order to achieve the purpose of your call, additional conversation is an opportunity for you to provide additional reasons for them to meet with you and tell them what they will get out of their first meeting for you.

Think about the "set the meeting" scripts that have been developed and used effectively to date. Although the words may differ, the formats of the winning scripts are essentially the same. You tell people who you are, where you are calling from, what you do, build credibility by dropping names of well known clients, then you relate the benefits that companies get by working with you... so you might mention, expertise, quick response, competitive pricing, some things that you do differently that companies have found helpful, unique programs you offer. You mention that you can provide them information, options and strategies regarding purchasing widgets and services that have proven valuable and helped companies reduce the burden or hassle of managing their widget purchases. Those are the benefits people get by agreeing to meet with you.

You then end by telling them exactly what you want them to do and asking them for the meeting. That is the successful formula for scoring a meeting. They can say "yes," they can say "no," or they offer some resistance that you must respond to.

The point is for you always to keep in mind that the

biggest reason why people don't agree to meet with you is because you don't give them enough reason to meet with you, and you don't ask for the meeting.

So when a prospect offers some resistance, you have to use this as an opportunity to provide them additional benefits or re-affirm the benefits they will get at the meeting, and again ask for the meeting. No matter where they want to go with the conversation, you always want to steer it back to restating the benefits they get by spending time with you, and asking for the meeting. This brings us right into the next concept for you to remember.

4. Always maintain control.

You always must maintain control over the conversation. If you lose control over the conversation, you are going to get caught in "maybe land." Once you lose control over the conversation, or let it drift away from your agenda, which is to book a meeting, you can only lose. How do you lose? You lose because then at best, ... You are into that "send me information, call me back, hey why don't you spend time to put together a quote for me even though the odds are high I won't purchase from you" space, and that is a very low productivity place to be in.

If you have read anything else by me or listened to me speak, you have probably heard me talk about the necessity of thinking in terms of "groups." Rather than caring about what happens on any individual call or whether you penetrate any individual account, worry much more about how effective you are with a similarly situated group of prospects. This is a good example of why you have to think in terms of groups.

If you concentrate on the individual, once they start talking about their standards, their issues, their challenges, whatever they bring up, the natural tendency is to think, "Well, this is important to them, I know a lot about that, I'll show them how smart I am and tell them the most important things right now."

But, if you do that you are actually making a couple of strategic errors. First, remember that gravity is working against you. Your target expects to decline your request for a meeting. The more you talk, the more opportunity you give them to conclude that a meeting would not be worth their time.

Second, if you answer their questions, they don't need you anymore. So why meet?

And third, when you respond in detail to what they say, you are now working on their agenda, and you have abandoned your agenda. If they take charge of the conversation, they are not going to lead you to a meeting. If any of those three things happen, you talk too much, you give out too much information, or you let them determine the course of the conversation, you can only lose.

How do you lose? You lose because almost always the result of the conversation will be "call me back, send me info, give me a quote on this even though we both know I probably won't buy anything." By your decisions and your actions, you have slotted that record into a group in which you know there is a low probability of success.

You want to be able to slot them into a group in which there is a much higher probability of success. And that

group is the group that has agreed to meet with you.
You maximize the odds that you schedule a meeting
if you maintain control of the conversation and always
come back to your agenda.

One other aside on the topic of maintaining control of
the conversation -- most successful conversations last
about 2 to 3 minutes. It is my opinion that you have to
try to steer the conversation to a successful conclusion
within that 2 to 3 minutes. If the conversation goes on
longer than that, the odds decrease that someone would
book a meeting with you. Why is that?

Well, you either give them the most valuable
information, don't give them enough reason to meet
with you, or the longer you talk the more opportunity
you give them to hang their hat on something to
conclude, "It's not worth my time to meet with this
person." Remember, they are expecting to conclude
that it is not worth their time to meet with you. If you
speak too long, you make it easier for them to make
that conclusion.

5. Every word counts.

You must ruthlessly eliminate unnecessary or wishy
washy words. You have a very short period of time
and are fighting gravity. Any word that is not directly
reinforcing why they should meet with you and what
they will get from that meeting should be eliminated.
Eliminate general mean nothing - waste of breath - just
fill up space when I can't think of anything meaningful
to say type phrases.

What are they? "We want to see what we can do for
you." "We want to tell you about the services we offer

and see if there is anything we can do to help you."

Anything you say that is non-specific and not related to communicating a benefit they will get at that meeting should be eliminated.

Once you have given it your best shot, you are better off to be silent than to fill space with wishy washy meaningless words.

6. How you say it matters.

It is not only what you say, but how you say it that counts. You want to be projecting a relaxed and confident demeanor. You are calling from a great company with a long list of good clients providing high quality products and services. Many you are calling are reviewing options from your competitors and many will be buying from your competitors within the next 6 months. It is the most natural and normal thing in the world for you to be calling companies and seeking a meeting. It would be the most normal natural thing in the world for them to agree to do so.

When in doubt speak in a clear, firm voice. Your prospect will almost always assume you know what you are talking about.

When you think and plan out in advance what words you will use to achieve your objective and you deliver those words naturally and confidently, without hemming and hawing, without hesitations, without uh, uh, uh, without throwing in needless and meaningless words, you greatly increase the odds that people will conclude that it would be worth spending time with you.

When you seem to be searching for words, hesitating, not quite sure of yourself on the phone, what do you think is going through your prospects' mind, "Well if this person isn't quite sure of what they want to say over the phone, how worthwhile would it be for me to meet with them?"

So much as you did with your set the meeting script, you want to think out in advance the best way to respond to resistance you will encounter and be ready for it. There are really only about a half dozen common scenarios you have to prepare for and when you recognize them, because you have pre-thought out in advance the best way to respond to them, it's like a big giant melon being pitched to you right over the plate and you are going to smash it right out of the park.

The 7 common forms of resistance you will encounter over the phone are as follows: "I'm all set, send some info, call me back, tell me, we are not buying right now, I get 20 calls a day from people like you, we buy Dell direct and lastly, I'll meet with you, but call me back in a month."

Before we go into specifically how you might best respond to these situations. One final comment. When you are prospecting, what you are really trying to do is re-shuffle the deck in order of priority. You identify your very best opportunities and schedule appointments with them, you identify your no opportunity or low probability targets and get rid of them, and then in the middle you have various shades of gray you have to prioritize and decide how much time to allocate to them.

For more script tips, samples and updates visit
www.AccordingToScott.com/script-extras

Chapter 13

Objection Response Scripts.

We are all set.

The "we are all set objection" sometimes expressed as we have a vendor we love, we have five vendors, we have a contract with 22 years left to run and it's unbreakable.

Here are 2 options to reply: "That's fine. Does that mean you are never going to look at new options or could you suggest a better time for me to call in the future?"

Or, reply to the "all set" objection with this... "That's fine. Look, we wouldn't expect anything to happen quickly anyway. That's not the way it happens in this business. We do an awful lot of business with companies like Mega Corp, International Amalgamated and Acme Intergalactic, and there are good reasons why companies like that decided to work with us. We would just be looking to introduce ourselves, give you some information on programs and strategies to make your process a bit easier, and if in the future you are looking for options or need a hard to source item, we would hope you think of us. Would that be worth 30 minutes of your time in the next few weeks?"

Let's look at the first response, "That's fine. Does that mean you are never going to look at new options or could you suggest a better time for me to call you in the future?"

What you are doing is giving your prospect the opportunity to reconfirm what they just told you and give you permission and direction as to when to call again.

You have no chance of getting a meeting with this response as you haven't given additional reasons why they should meet with you and you haven't asked for the meeting again. This response is probably best when you have someone who is very gruff or appears rushed and you don't feel you can give the longer response.

My opinion is that you should try some variation of the longer response.

"That's fine. Look, we wouldn't expect anything to happen quickly anyway. That's not the way it happens in this business. We do an awful lot of business with companies like Mega Corp, International Amalgamated and Acme Intergalactic, and they selected us because they save time, administrative headaches and costs. We would just be looking to introduce ourselves, give you some information on programs and strategies to make your process a bit easier. If in the future you are looking for options, we would hope you think of us. Would that be worth 30 minutes of your time in the next few weeks?"

What you are doing with this script is to lower their expectations and reassure them that you are not asking them to change. You then re-establish your credibility by mentioning how much business you do and then drop the names of more great companies that have chosen to do business with you. Notice the phrases "other companies have chosen us" "and expertise." These are the little things you drop to convey benefits and convince someone it would be worth their time to meet with you.

Then you end up telling them what they will get at that meeting -- not in the future -- but at that meeting. You say something like, "We will give you some information on X, Y and Z and some strategies to make your process a bit easier." You then go for the close by saying something like "If in the future you are looking for options or need to source a hard to find item, we hope you think of us. Would that be worth 30 minutes of your time" or, your final line can be, "If that is worth 30 minutes of your time, would you be available on April 1st or 2nd?"

If you feel comfortable with it, the second question, "If that is worth 30 minutes of your time, would you be available on April 1st or 2nd?" is better because they need to say "yes" only once.

So what you have done is kept control of the conversation, given them additional reasons to meet with you and asked for the meeting. If they say "no," then you can ask them to suggest a good time for you to call them.

Send me some information.
Are you a wimp?

Now let's discuss the "send me some information" objection. Probably the most common thing you will hear.

Let me be blunt. If your response to "send me some information" is "um, OK". You are a wimp and you are dooming yourself to prospecting frustration and wasting a lot of time and company resources.

We know that 9 times out of 10, at least, when someone says, "Send me some information," it is really a blow-off. Rather than tell you to get lost, they mumble a request to send them something and for them the phone call is over.

But if you let the caller control the call, you lose. Because now you have doomed yourself to calling back, calling back, banging your head against the wall, and getting frustrated that these people who asked for information, who you think might be legitimately interested, don't return your calls, and if after 10 or 15 attempts if you do get them back on the phone, almost always, they at best vaguely remember you. If they did get something they haven't read it, and that's if they remember receiving it all.

If you get on this treadmill it is your fault, not the fault of the people you are targeting. Remember that your objective in prospecting is not just to set sales appointments, it is to re-shuffle the deck and sort your prospects in accordance with their potential value and worth. If you just say "ok" to the send more information blow-off, you have received no information of value to you. Not only that, even those people who are legitimately high potential, high value, we are looking for a new vendor, "we have a big order coming up and are willing to look at options type prospects," are not given the opportunity to identify themselves to you.

If you don't give the higher-value more likely to buy sooner than later types of prospects the opportunity to identify themselves to you, you won't know who they are and you won't know who is worth more of your time.

The next time you get the send more information blow-off, consider saying something like this. "You know, I don't send out general information. The general corporate stuff I might send you is going to tell you what I just told you. We are a $90 million dollar company that's been in business 15 years supplying technology equipment like widgets and wadgets to companies like United Intergalactic, Mega Corp and I B Sorry Corp. If there is some specific information that would be helpful to you, if you happen to have a specific purchase coming up or would like some info on something specific, I would be happy to put it together and send it out to you. Do you have anything specific in mind that I can help you with?"

And at that point you do the most difficult thing for a salesperson to do. You say nothing and wait for your prospect to speak.

If they can't come up with something specific, then because you have given them the opportunity to give you enough information so that you can properly slot them, you can go right into plan B and cut them loose.

With that response you can identify the tire-kickers and non-buyers. No follow-up calls to them. No money spent on them. Because you are prepared and know what to say to accomplish your business objectives, that time and those resources will be allocated to a higher probability prospect.

If they do come up with something specific, say something to the effect,... "Well, you know we are going to replace $500,000 worth of widgets in a month, or we are going to buy $1,200,000 worth of stuff next quarter, why don't you send me some info on x ,y or z..."

Now you know you have a live one and you have to do 3 things.

First you have to really listen. Let them speak. Don't interrupt. When they are done, you ask a couple of open ended questions to clarify their request and allow them to give you more information on their needs.

And then you come back to your agenda. Remember, we started out by saying that you never let your target's agenda become your agenda. They may be asking you for information but you need a meeting. You, in particular, know that the odds of landing an account go up substantially when you get a meeting.

So when a target has told you they have a specific need or purchase coming up, it is even more important that you land a meeting with them. Remember the biggest reasons why people don't meet with you is that you don't give them enough reason to meet with you and you don't ask.

So after listening to their request, then clarifying it with a couple of open ended questions, you then swing it back to your agenda and say something like this.

"You know, I could put together a lot of info that would be useful to you...right off the top of my head I can think of 3 companies in your industry we helped to select and install what you seem to be looking for. I don't know a lot of details about your company, but you have a few options to consider on this and there are a couple of things you want to avoid that could really cost you some money. You know, Super Salesperson is our rep in your area and he has a lot of experience with this. If he had the opportunity to learn more specifics about your company he could give you a lot of information that would be helpful to you and specific to your situation. It may or may not lead to a next step. Either is fine. I could set a meeting for you now. Would that be worth 30 minutes of your time?"

With this structure, you can effectively identify the qualified and, kick the time-wasters to the curb.

So let's look at what you have done. You have given those companies that do have a specific need the opportunity to inform you of that need. You have leveraged that info into a tremendous benefit that they will receive if they agree to meet with you. They will get specific information on their specific needs from someone who is very knowledgeable. That is a reason for people to meet with you.

If they say "yes," you book it Dano, if they say "no," you tell them you will send out the info and ask when you should follow up.

When they say "no." Always say this.

When they have turned you down repeatedly, before you hang up, always say this.

"No problem, don't want to be on your back, but obviously we do an awful lot of this. Could you suggest a time to call you in the future?'

Now do the hardest thing for a salesperson to do. Shut up.

You will be shocked how many people will say to you "call me in a month." Or "call me at the end of next quarter."

When they do you follow up with this. "Sure, happy to do that. Is there a particular reason why that is a good time to call?"

They will tell you and a dead-end call turns into a real opportunity.

Always end your calls with this. You will be surprised how many fish jump back into the boat.

Two Other Points

Now before we get off the send more info objection, I would like you to keep 2 other points in mind.

First, sometimes your greatest strength can be your greatest weakness. It is very difficult for someone who has a lot of knowledge in a particular area to withhold information when they are talking to a prospect. But that is exactly what you have to do at this stage of the process.

What you decide to withhold is as important as what you decide to say. If you provide too much information, you give them the opportunity to conclude that they should not meet with you. Every bone in their body is looking for a reason not to meet with you and when the conversation lasts more than 2 or 3 minutes, you will probably give them something to hang their hat on. Also, if you talk too much, you are talking about their agenda and not your agenda, and you can only lose in that space.

Also, notice what did not happen during this conversation. As soon as the rep heard about a potential purchase they did not, fall into "Hey, what are your standards, give me more specifics on your order, let me run around and put together a quote for you mode." Do not do this.

You know that when you just give a quote for a substantial order to a company you haven't met you have only a very very slight chance of converting that into an account. When you meet with someone and then provide a quote you have a 1 in 5 to a 1 in 8 chance of gaining an account.

If you have a live one, in what zone would you like to work? With a 1 in 100 chance that they will become an account, or with a 1 in 5 chance that they become an account? If you drop into "let me put a quote together for you mode too quickly" it is by your decision and your actions that at best put this into the quote category, when it might have been in the meeting category.

Make every effort to schedule the meeting first and make sure they tell you they don't want to schedule a meeting before you go to "Plan B" or "when should I call you next" territory.

Call me back

Now on to common objection number 3, the call me back objection. Let me give you some things to think about with this.

Again, the vast majority of the time this is a blow- off. If you just say "ok" and act in accordance with their agenda, you lose. You know that you are doomed to making call after call and getting nowhere. You have them on the phone now. You need some information to properly slot them, so that you can decide whether you will call them back.

I would recommend that you proceed as follows: "I would be happy to do that, when would you suggest I call you? Once they give you a time period you say, "I would be happy to contact you then. Is there a specific reason why that's a good reason to call you then?"

They will then tell you essentially 1 of 2 things. They will give you a general, "I am busy now" or "there is nothing happening" type response. Or they will give you a specific response with information that is helpful to your agenda, which is to find out whether you have a realistic chance of making a sale.

That specific response will typically be something like, " Well, we are planning to buy a $1billion worth of product or services you sell and I will have the specs then." Or, "I know we are going to review our vendors then and I would like to hear about your company" or, "I'm in the middle of month end, quarter end, year end and won't be able to focus on our needs in this area until then."

Once you get a valid legitimate reason and know that you have a viable prospect, you can end up by saying, "Thank you very much, I will contact you then. One quick question: how many employees do you have or how many users do you have, or how many employee relocations do you do every year, or how many salespeople do you have?" They give the response and you end by saying, "Talk to you in two months." Click.

Now if they give you a very generic, non-specific reason or say, "I just don't have time for this right now." There is something you have to know. Is this a run me around the block, time wasting, no need, go nowhere prospect who thinks you are just going to call and call and call on their whim, and who is going to suck every bit of motivation and energy out of your body by having you chase them and get nothing for your time and effort,...

Or , is this someone who legitimately would welcome a call from you for a legitimate reason. You can find out now, or you can find out 10 phone calls from now.

So if you have some guts, see if you could bring yourself to say something like this: "You know, I would be happy to call you back... but look, we provided companies like, x, y and z, about $100 million worth of widgets and wadgets and we are doing quite well. I don't want to be on your back. If you are not open to a new source of supply, just tell me and I won't bother you. "

Now, if you say something like that, they will either say something like, "Well, I really am not going to have anything for you," to which you can ask, "Not an issue. Don't want to be on your back. When would you suggest I be back in touch?" They tell you. You say "Thankyouverymuch." Click.

Or, they will say something to the effect, "Oh no, I want you to call me. We are looking for this. We might buy that." To which you respond, "That's great. Call you in 2 months. Thankyouverymuch." Click.

Now let's look at what you have done with a few simple, direct questions asked with surgical precision. In any group of 100 send me some information responses, we know that 90 or more of them are blow-offs. At best, 10 of them may lead to a legitimate opportunity. You have them on the phone now. Ask the questions and separate the time wasters from the legitimate opportunities.

If they are in the time waster category, the conversation goes something like this after your 30 second set the meeting script is delivered.

"Sure, I would be happy to call you back. Is there a specific reason why you want me to call you at that time?"

Or,

"Oh, well I would be happy to call you but look, we provide companies like x, y, and z with about $100 million worth of technology equipment a year, I don't want to be on your back if you don't have a need or don't plan on looking at vendor options. Do you really think it would be worthwhile for me to call you in 2 months or not? It's perfectly OK for you to tell me it won't be."

My opinion is that it's a whole lot easier to learn how to get those few simple questions out and get the information you need, rather than get frustrated, de-motivated, and poorer because you let people run you around the flagpole and waste your time.

Now the balance of the common objections are as follows: The "tell me" objection, the "I get 20 calls like this a day" objection, the "home office is in Beirut objection," and the "I'll meet with you but call me in a month" objection. All the responses fall into a familiar pattern and we can cover them quickly.

Call me back.

First, the "I'll meet with you but call me in a month objection." Keep in mind that approximately half of those who specifically tell you they will meet with them but ask you to call them back, will actually book a meeting with you. Half. And that half usually only books it after you get them on the phone again, no small achievement.

So if their mindset is that they will meet with you at some time, give it a shot to book a meeting now, rather than later. The conversations would go something like this: "Sure, I would be happy to call you then. We would probably be looking to get together a few weeks after that, so that would put us into the week of April 15. You know, we are in your area quite frequently and I know I would schedule a few other visits on the

same trip. If you feel comfortable, would you mind if
we penciled something in the week of April 15 or so.
It would help me with my planning, and I would call
you a week before to make sure the time still works for
you. Would you feel comfortable doing that?"

 Book it if they say yes, tell them you will call them in
a month if they say no.

Tell me

 Now on to the "tell me" objection, which usually rears
its head with words like "who are you or what do you
do." Your best response is to tell them what you have
already told them, and again ask for the meeting.

 "We work with companies like International
Amalgamated, Acme Intergalactic and Humongous
Corporation. They selected us to provide about $90
million worth of widgets and use us because they save
time, administrative headaches, and costs. We want
to introduce ourselves and tell you about some things
we do differently in providing widgets that other
companies have found valuable. Our private inventory
or maximarketplace programs may have some benefits
for you and I'm asking for 30 minutes to give you that
information. If you think of us in the future that would
be great. Would you have some time in a few weeks,
say April 28 or 29?"

 Don't delve into other areas or provide them new
information because all you do is give them too much
to process and too much to think about. Remember,
if there is any doubt in their mind, they will not agree
to meet with you. Providing additional credibility
statements and again telling them the benefits they

would get at a meeting, if they met with you, is the best course.

20 calls a day.

The "I get 20 calls like this a day objection." Well, first of all, that objection only tells you what you already know. That many teleprospectors who are not as talented as you have called. You also know that every bone and muscle in the body of your target is expecting to say "no" to you. That is the common knee jerk response.

You must fight gravity in this situation and cut through all the pre-conceived notions in your prospects head as to why they should deny your request. Your response would be very similar to the "tell me" response.

"Look, I don't want to be on your back. We are a $90 million company and companies like A, B and C have selected us to source their widget equipment. I don't know if we might help you, but we do a few things differently that companies find save them time, administrative headaches and costs, and have a couple of unique programs like private inventory and maxi-marketplace that a lot of companies have found helpful. If getting info on strategies that have proven valuable to similar companies is worth 30 minutes of your time, that would be great. If not, that is fine also. Would you have some time in the next week or 2?"

So what have you done? Re-established your credibility and told them about some powerful benefits they get if they meet with you. You also ignored their agenda, which is to moan about people calling them, a fact which is meaningless to us, and kept the conversation on your agenda.

You have steered the conversation so that you get a clear yes or no, and then can go onto your next call. Remember also that just because a lot of people have called them doesn't mean you don't have a shot at getting a meeting. Most telemarketers are pretty poor, and you are much better than average, so you can succeed where others fail.

The home office makes all the decisions.

The "home office makes all the decisions" objection, and they are located in Beirut, is pretty straightforward. All you can really do is ask if they can tell you who to send information to in Beirut who is in charge of purchasing widget equipment, and then ask them, if there is anyone at their site who has input into such decisions that they would recommend you send some info to. They will either give you the names or they won't, and you can decide to follow up or not.

So again, with your response you establish credibility, tell them the benefits they will get if they agree to meet with you and ask for the meeting.

Now most of the time, even if you are very very good at setting sales appointments, the real world is that most people will say "no." That does not mean you cannot achieve the purpose of your call. We are prospecting, not simply appointment setting, and an additional purpose of the call is to sort our suspects in order of priority. The suspects you talk to might have a need in the near future, and the odds are certainly that at some time in the future they will buy something from somebody and virtually every company at some time re-evaluates their vendor relationships.

For more script tips, samples and updates visit
www.AccordingToScott.com/script-extras

Chapter 14

Phrases of Shame

Commonly used words self-sabotage your prospecting efforts and snatch defeat from the jaws of sales victory.

Why do people work so hard to call, call, call to get Ms. Top Decision Maker on the phone... only to use words that are the equivalent of hitting their suspects with a baseball bat. No wonder they get blown off and the suspects run away. By their own words they have caused that to happen.

Let me share some of the nutty, ridiculous, time wasting, say nothing, just lump me in with all the other idiots that call you and waste your time -- things that people say that chase away qualified prospects they have worked very hard to get on the phone.

Can you believe that people actually open up their calls with things like...

How are you?

Have you got a minute?

I'll be brief.

I'll only take 20 minutes of your time.

I'm calling to follow-up on a letter (or package) sent.

Why is this nuts? The first few seconds of the call are critical to them deciding you are worthwhile to talk to. If you are not perceived to be credible or touch some hot button you might help them with, you are toast.

What does saying those things do to contribute to their knowledge of how you might help them or that you have enough credibility worth investing some time?

Nothing. They contribute nothing. So don't say them.

"How are you?" You don't know them. They don't know you. Could this be less sincere?

"Have you got a minute?" Again, if they don't know you, what you might help them with or how credible you are, why should they have any time for you. Don't ask them for time until you have laid the proper foundation.

"I'll be brief." That is not a benefit or something worthwhile. The fact that you will only waste a little bit of their time does not score points. Plus, dozens of callers have said the same thing to them before and then ramble on endlessly, so they don't buy it.

But the biggest reason saying things like that are self-destructive is they communicate nothing about your value or what you do. If the person you are talking to has a need you can fulfill.... you are giving them absolutely no information that enables them to conclude that you are worth listening to.

Another blunder...

I'm just calling to follow-up on a letter/package sent to you.

Why is this nuts? We discussed previously that the response you get 99.9% of the time is... "I didn't get it... I didn't read it. Please send it again." So now, by your own choice of words you have immolated yourself. The call is over. Why would anyone do that?

If you have the decision maker on the phone use words that will sell the meeting. Don't choose words that are guaranteed to throw the conversation off course.

"I'd like to stop by and see you and will only take 20 minutes."

This is a very self-destructive statement for 2 reasons. First, if you have nothing worthwhile to offer them the fact you will only take 20 minutes is not a benefit. Second, people buy from peers. What you are communicating with this statement is that their time is more valuable than yours.

Bottom line. Don't say things to lower your perceived value. If they have an issue with time, let them bring it up.

"Can I call back and check with you in a month?"

This is a great example of doing all the work and getting no results. Don't ever suggest a time to call them back. Always let them suggest a time. Enable them to tell you how you can sell them. You learn nothing from them if you say that.

A better approach... "No problem... don't want to be on your back... but obviously we do a lot of this, can you suggest a better time to get back in touch with you?" Then be quiet. Let them tell you. When they do say something like this... "Happy to call you then, may I ask why that is a good time?"

See the difference? The first approach gives you no information to separate the hot prospects from the time wasters. By your own choice of words you doom yourself to following up on multiples of people that will never buy. With the second approach, you enable them to tell you if they have a need and when it will be actionable.

Keep these 2 points in mind. You always want to communicate value and enable them to tell you how to sell them. Rip out any words that don't directly contribute to those two objectives.

Never use these words.

Avoid/minimize "We" and "I." It's all about your prospect/suspect. Not you. They don't care about you. Only what they will get from you.

Do not say things like this:

"I'm calling regarding..."
"The reason for my call is..."

Wasted words. Get to the point. Just say it.

"With our system..."
"We have been able to..."
"I would like to..."

Get rid of the "I" and "we" orientation. Rephrase to a "you" orientation. "What you get," "others have achieved," "You will hear."

"....give you a comprehensive proposal..."
Shoot yourself if you ever say this in an initial "set the meeting" discussion.

.
"Would Monday morning or Thursday afternoon be best for you?

Shoot yourself again. Overused. Immediately flags you as a newbie. If you say this after your inital 30-second sript and they say "no." You don't know whether they object to those times or your overall value proposition. So how can you respond properly? Use "Do you have any time in the next week or two."

"We want to meet with you for 10 minutes"
The lies begin and your suspect knows it. Your sincerity meter just plummeted. A short meeting is not a benefit if you have nothing to say. If you have true value, state it and let the suspect voice any length of meeting concerns. Also, by your own words you are diminishing your value. You have just verbally immolated yourself.

"Companies just like yours..."
Suspects immediately discount you significantly when you say this. You have not met with them. You

do not know their needs and issues until you meet. Phrases like this self-sabotage your credibility and perceived value.

"I'm trying to find out how many salespeople you have. I want to send out some newsletters and don't want to chop down extra trees. For curiosities sake, how many salespeople do you have in all location?"

Real bad. An "I" orientation. Way too much information. Confusing. Simplify it and get to the point. "Just so I know what to send, about how many salespeople do you have?" Then be quiet. No extra words.

"We help companies select _____ that best meet their needs."
Wow, that's unique. Boring. Says nothing. A bit dumb.

For more script tips, samples and updates visit
www.AccordingToScott.com/script-extras

Chapter 15

Key Scripting Strategies and Concepts.

There is a bigger picture that your script structures and phone behaviors must be consistent with in order to succeed.

Here are some top principles I believe in strongly.

A. There are many reasons why someone might meet with you. They want to buy is only 1.

Don't limit your script strategizing to thinking that someone will meet with you because they may wish to do business with you. Far from it.

There are many reasons why people might meet with you and you want to appeal to as many of these reasons as you can in your scripts and responses to objections.

- Curiosity
- Personal benefit
- Not wanting to be left out
- Don't want the boss to yell at them
- Fear of being wrong
- Afraid of competition
- Gain an advantage over a co-worker
- Gain power or influence
- Keep their job
- Oh yeah, some meet because they want to buy

Remember, you need to meet with a qualified buyer to have any chance of making a sale. No meeting. No sale.

Activate as many of the above motivations as possible to get that meeting.

B. Don't try to convince people of anything.

Right now, there are people and companies thinking about and in the process of purchasing exactly what it is that you are selling. Many just completed purchases with competitors and you weren't there. Many will buy from competitors within the next three to 12 months. Where will you be?

When I called, my goal was simply to bump into someone that recognized they had a need and with compelling words enable them to conclude that it was worth spending more time with a representative of my client company. That's it.

Don't place the burden on yourself to convince people of anything. Find people that already have it within them on some level to take action on what you are offering. When you bump into them, say the things that enable them to realize you are worth some of their time. Don't screw it up.

3. Think "Groups."

You make 1 call at a time but you must think in terms of groups. You select groups to call. You encounter distinct groups of similar scenarios you must respond to.

You select groups with similar characteristics to call and rank them by priority. Call the most responsive and worthwhile first based upon your time and resources available.

You run into similar scenarios all the time. Decision makers pick up the phone and say "hello." You get voicemail a lot. You hear certain objections or questions a lot. Gatekeepers ask you the same things over and over.

When you are on the phone and hear "send me some info," you are not trying to "win" on that phone call as much as you are trying to use the words and behaviors that you know are most successful in accomplishing your business objective with that "group" of objections.

As long as you are saying the words and behaving consistent with the actions that are most likely to be successful with a certain group of scenarios you run into, that is what matters.

What happens on any one call does not matter.

What matters is your relative success handling a similar group of call scenarios.

You can't control what happens on the other end of the line. You can only control what you do.

Do you convert 1 in 3 conversations to a meeting or 1 in 10?

Do you overcome the "send me info" objection 10% of the time or 30% of the time?

Think not of success with any one call, but think of success among a similar group of calls.

So long as your words and behaviors were consistent with the approach most likely to get you success with that scenario, you had a successful call. You will get the best results and you stop worrying about what happens on any one call.

3. Researching is ridiculous.

I set more than 2,000 C-Level sales appointments. I never once did any research on a company before I called.

I know it is common wisdom and the great unwashed accept it as gospel, but it has always hit me as nuts.

These are my thoughts:

When you work a call process with a carefully selected group of companies that fit a specific profile... size, industry, similar needs, hot buttons and other factors.... you call, call, call to get X results.

So, for example, you call 20 hours a week to get 7 meetings.

You now decide to "research" before you call. That research now means you spend 10 hours calling and 10 hours researching. Researching has to double your results just to break even. Never happens.

I have another reason, other than simple math, as to why I think researching individual companies as a matter of course is ridiculous. It hardly ever uncovers anything significant that you can say that increases your odds of getting a meeting.

But wait. There's more. Those who think researching is helpful to them in getting more appointments misunderstand what is happening on the calls.

It is not what you know about them that gets you a meeting. It is what they perceive you may be able to do for them that get you a meeting. You are not trying to close on a final purchase, just the first step. A meeting.

You research the needs and wants of the group you are calling so that your core script gets you 7 meetings a week and not 5, or 3 or 1 with the same time investment.

You need meetings with top decision makers at companies that are clones of your best accounts. The more meetings with qualified decision makers you get the more you will sell.

"Researching" individual companies will typically decrease the number of qualified appointments you schedule with the same time investment.

For more script tips, samples and updates visit
www.AccordingToScott.com/script-extras

Chapter 16

Sample Scripts and Component Parts

Here are sample scripts and sample language you might use in your scripts. The script samples will give you language you may use but most importantly serve as examples of the script structures you should use. The component part sample language should stimulate your thinking as to phrases that would work for you.

Identify the decision-maker scripts

"I am looking to send some information to the (insert title.)" Can you tell me who to direct it to?"

"I'm looking to send some information to the purchasing agent that handles _____ components. Can you tell me who to direct it to?"

"HI, I'm looking to send a package to whomever

heads the engineering department. Can you tell me who to direct it to?"

"Hi, I would like to send some information to whoever is in charge of cash management or treasury management. Could you tell me who to direct it to?"

Sample core "set the appointment" scripts

"Hi, this is _____ from Better Benefits Corporation. We specialize in helping companies select and manage employee benefit plans. Over 500 companies in the Fargo area work with us to control their health insurance costs without reducing core benefits. Our proprietary data analytics and predictive modeling tools have proven to reduce overall benefit costs. We would like to introduce ourselves and relate the methods and strategies that others have found effective in controlling their benefit costs. Would you have some time in the next week or two?"

"This is Chatty from Super Performance Group. We specialize in sales team performance improvement. Companies like Mega Corp, I. B. Sorry and Joe's Garage have selected us as they get reduced sales team turnover, value communication strategies and reduced time to close. (Note: other benefits that might be mentioned are "increased average sale size'" "higher conversion rates" or "faster time to close." I have no idea if you might be looking for information or strategies regarding closing more accounts. If you are, we would like the opportunity to introduce ourselves and share some options other companies have found valuable. There may or may not be a next step, either is fine. If you think of us in the future, that would be great. Would you have some time in the next week or two?"

"This is Lee from Super Services. We specialize in developing web-based education systems. Companies such as HV, Microsquishy and Brito Unlimited have chosen us to get 30% sales growth, expanded market share and deployment in about 10 weeks. If you are open to reviewing some new options and strategies, I'd like to introduce myself and share some specific case studies and examples as to how these results have been achieved. You will definitely learn some things and we hope you think of us in the future. Would you have some time in the next week or two?"

"This is Billy Bob with Medical Magic. We help companies manage health insurance spend while increasing employee benefits with strategies such as _____ and _____. Companies like U. B. Sorry Financial, Fleecem and How, and Dewey Screwem have worked with us. Average first year savings are $120,000 and one new client saved $970,000 last year. There have been some legislative changes and we would like to introduce ourselves and share with you some insight and program options many firms have found valuable. When the time comes to evaluate your program you will have up to date info and case studies to make your best decision. If you think of us down the road that would be great. Would you have some time in the next week or two?"

" This is Howie from Mega Money. Our wealth management practice is exclusive to those with a $7 million net worth. 18 families work with us as they get a 3 to 1 client to staff ratio, specialized knowledge and complete information as to all options. If you are open to reviewing some options and strategies to maximize assets that have been appreciated by others we would like to introduce ourselves. If you think of us in the future that would be great. Would you have some time in the next week or two?"

"This is _____ from Mega Corp. We specialize in _____. More than 200 leading brands including _____, _____, and _____ have selected us over better known competitors as they typically get 5% improvement in _____, reduce _____ by 10% and quickly realize bottom line profit by about $4 per transaction. If you are open to reviewing unique processes that enable you to reduce _____ , control _____ and obtain _____, I would like to introduce myself and share specific technologies that drive value across departments. You will definitely learn a few things and we hope you think of us in the future. Would you have some time in the next week or two?"

" Hi this is _____ from VerySmart Company. We provide education technology solutions and been selected by school systems such as _____, _____ , _____ and 2,200 others. They select us as they get benefit A, Benefit B and Benefit C. If you are open to reviewing popular options in classroom technology I would like to introduce myself and and share specific examples of how other school systems are achieving these objectives. I know you will learn a few things and get hands on experience with the technology. Do you have some time in the next week or two?"

"This is Bill with North States Copper. We specialize

in custom fabricated extrusions. Companies like Mega Company #1, Mega Company #2 and Mega Company #3 work with us to get a 99% quality rating, 97% on time and complete delivery and short lead times. Have no idea if you might be willing to review some options. If so, we would love to introduce ourselves and share with you specific processes and strategies others have used to improve delivery time, quality and costs. Would you have some time in the next week or two?"

"This is Kelly from Payne International. We are copper mining productivity specialists. More than half of the global mining companies including _____, _____ and _____ have selected us for more than 200 engagements over the last 5 years. They work with us to eliminate capital project overruns, increase throughput on average about 20% and reduce unit costs. Have no idea if you wish to review options and strategies other mining companies have used to achieve these results. If so, I'd like to meet with you and discuss specifics of the various strategies. You will pick up some good ideas and if you think of us in the future that would be great. Would you have some time in the next week or two?"

"HI, this is Kelly from ABC group. We are workplace design, construction and furnishing specialists. More than 1,000 offices including Well Known Name and Locally Recognized Name B have selected us to maximize productivity and showcase their success with workplaces that are ergonomic, energy efficient, impressive and on-budget. If you have any type of workplace improvement on your horizon we would like to introduce ourselves and share specific examples and case studies. You will definitely learn something about workplace design and we hope you think of us in the future."

DESCRIBING WHAT YOU DO

We specialize

Provide technology solutions
Bring interactive technology into the _____
Specialize in integration of technology into _____

We are business management consultants.
We are copper mining productivity specialists.

CREDIBILITY

"... more than 850 in Chicago have tried..."

"...#1 in the nation..."

"...do more business than the #2 - #5 competitors combined..."

"400,000 seniors have selected us."

"19,000 senior homeowners last year..."

"... more than 200 leading brands including A, B and C..."

"...more than 200 leading brands trust us to..."

"... 6% improvement in customer retention..."

"... drive incremental value across departments ..."

"More than 5,000 schools have selected us for

sourcing of..."

"... chosen by more than 6 million families ..."

"Over 500 companies in the _____ area. (city, state, county)"

"More than 100 leading brands including _____, _____ and _____ ..."

"Companies like _____, _____ and _____."

"Fortune 500 companies like †_____ and _____."

"More than 300 families in the Wazoo area have selected us..."

"We are #1 in the midwest and #3 in the country."

Service 24 countries.

61% of school systems in Ohio.

Drop names of companies that you have done business with.

"14 Fortune 500 companies in Georgia work with us."

"... service more than 2 gazillion corporate clients worldwide..."

"... thousands of homeowners..."

"Last year 220 companies.... (or homeowners.)"

BENEFITS

Predictable costs.

Simplify invoices.

Cut process time by 22%.

Elimination of coverage gaps.

Achieve 4 - 25% annual expense reductions.

11X more efficient .

3 hour response time.

Productivity gains.

Personal productivity.

Unlock full productivity.

Improve productivity.

Productivity and business efficiency.

Cost certainty.

Avoid business interruption.

Competitive pricing.

Less down time.

Less unscheduled disruption.

Faster restore time.

Handle overflow of work.

Resource for specialized services.

Reduce administration cost.

Business agility.

Accelerate.

Reduce.

Regulatory compliance.

Employee engagement.

Increase end-user productivity.

Competitive advantage.

Retain best talent.

Improve time to market.

Unleash business growth.

More efficient.

Scalability

Operational efficiencies.
Streamline the process.

Streamline the process for 900,000 employees/users.

Expert collaboration on design process.

96% on-time and complete delivery.

Short lead times.

Reduction of cost.

Reduce complexity.

Scalable.

Cost certainty.

Avoid business interruption.

Less unscheduled interruption.

WHAT DO THEY GET AT THE MEETING

"Would you be open to discussing..."

"If you are open to reviewing some options and strategies..."

"If you are open to exploring some new options and strategies..."

"If you are considering..."

"If you are open to reviewing processes to manage business productivity...."

"... share options and strategies..."

"I would like to introduce myself and share with

you..."

"...introduce myself and share ideas welcomed by many..."

"...relate methods and strategies..."

"...if you wish to review strategies used by others to achieve results like this, we would be happy to share pro's and con's of options you might select and common pitfalls you need to avoid..."

"... whether you just want to listen to new ideas or may have a change initiative coming up, we would be happy to share this information and hope you think of us in the future..."

"If you are open to reviewing some _____ strategies that hundreds of companies have chosen over better known competitors...."

"... open to reviewing specific process case studies..."

"... share with you some specific examples..."

"... share with you specific examples of technology projects that impacted profits..."

"... would like to share information re your needs and our capabilities." (Loved saying this.)

"... review some _____ strategies that hundreds of companies have chosen over better known competitors..."

"... share some specific practices..."

"... demonstrate some specific examples of customized interactive _____ methods..."

"... share specific examples of _____ projects that impacted profits..."

"... share with you specific information, samples, strategies, case histories others..."

"Would you be open to learning how _____ and _____ achieved these results..."

"... share with you specific information, case studies and strategies as to how other companies have ..."

"... share with you some samples, methods, programs others have found effective..."

"... discuss specific fiscal and plan design strategies..."

"... others have found effective..."

"... you are guaranteed to get a lot of helpful information...'

"...give you some information and strategies other firms have used to recover costs and enhance productivity..."

"We would like to introduce ourselves and share specific examples and strategies employed by others to maximize employee productivity, minimize downtime and stay within budget."

"...you can be informed of best technology options so when your time comes to _____ you will make the best decision for your company."

VOICEMAILS

"If E-payment software for banks that attract new business and fee income in select industries such as real estate, non-profits and B2B is worth exploring, Mega Financial, Bob's Bank and more than 200 others have realized increased market share and revenue streams and we would be happy to share specifics. This is Billy Bob with Payments Plus. 978-123-4567. Billy Bob, 978-123-4567."

"26 business owners with net worth over $5 million have selected our wealth management practice to get _____. Happy to share some options and strategies that have proven valuable to others in this environment. This is Sally Salesperson with Ultra Financial. 977-123-4567. Sally salesperson. 977-123-4567."

"Are your _____ strategies keeping up with the competition? More than 200 leading brands including A, B and C get increased customer retention, incremental purchases and reduce costs by 20 - 30%. Would be hapy to share info re your needs and why we are chosen over better known competitors. This is Chatty from Mega Corp, 211-123-4567. Chatty 211-123-4567."

"Looking for ERP options to improve productivity? Results recently achieved include reductions in month end close by 70% and order cycle time by 25%. More than 200 companies including _____, _____ and _____ selected us and would be happy to share with you program options and strategies proven successful. This is Lee Payne from Megatech. 978-123-4567. Lee 978-123-4567."

"If you are open to new extrusion component options, companies like Meganame1, Meganame2 and Meganame3 selected us to meet their engineering, delivery and cost requirements. Happy to share specifics. This is Joanna lee from North Shore Manufacturing 978-123-4567. Joanna Lee. 978-123-4567."

"If there is a workplace design or construction project on your horizon more than 1,000 Chicago area offices have chosen us to maximize productivity and the look of success with energy efficient rebuilds that are on-budget and coordinated from conception to grand opening. We would be happy to share information on your needs and our capabilities. This is Kelly from ABC group. 123-456-7890. Kelly. 123-456-7890."

Total Script Path Sample #1

"Hi, I would like to send some information to whoever handles the business insurance. Could you tell me who to direct it to?

Would you mind if I emailed that? What is the email address?

Just so I know what to send, do you have a rough idea how many employees there are in the company?

Thankyouverymuchclick.

"Hi, this is _____ with Mega Insurance. We

specialize in helping contractors with business insurance. More than 300 contractors on the North Shore, including _____ and _____ have selected us, as they get special programs, industry expertise and competitive pricing. I have no idea if you might be open to reviewing some options to improve coverage and reduce gaps that could cost you money. If so, I would like to introduce myself and share a number of specific program options. If you think of us in the future that would be great. Would you have some time in the next week or two?"

Send some info objection

"We don't send out general information as it will just repeat what I said. For 25 years we have specialize in helping contractors with their business insurance needs and hundreds work with us including _____ and _____. There are good reasons why so many work with us after reviewing all their options. If there is something specific you want I would be happy to put together something that will actually be of assistance to you. Is there something specific that you wish information on?"

We are all set objection

"That is fine, even if we got together we wouldn't expect anything to happen quick. That is not how it happens in this business. More than 300 contractors on the North Shore work with us as they get special industry programs, expertise and more coverage for less cost. If we did get together we would share with you specifics as to some unique service programs others find helpful. If in the future you have a specialized need or wish to review vendors you'll have a great resource. We hope you think of us. If that is worth 30 minutes would you have time next Thursday or Friday, the 12 or 13th?"

"Not a problem. We wouldn't expect anything to happen quickly. We do a lot of this, are #1 in the midwest and have been chosen by more than 1,200 college. We would like to share with you specific examples of how test scores were improved and class prep time decreased. You would be informed of all technology options so that when it is time to upgrade your facility you would make the best decision for your school. I'm looking at my calendar, would next week work?"

They still say "no."

"That is fine. Don't want to be on your back. Does that mean you will never look at program options or could you suggest a better time to be back in touch?"

"Great. Happy to call you then. Is there a particular reason why that is a good time to call you?"

"Thankyouverymuch." Click.

Total Script Path #2

"Hi, this is Joanna from McGehee Contracting. Since 1976 thousands in Beverly, Danvers and surrounding areas have selected us for siding, roofing, kitchen and bath projects as they get complete information on all options and pricing choices, experienced advice and professional workmanship. If a repair, upgrade or energy efficiency project might be in your future we would like to introduce ourselves and provide you with specifics as to grades, styles and trends. You would get expert advice from a 20 year professional in home improvements, an on the spot quote, financing and a lifetime guarantee. There is no obligation and you are guaranteed to get a lot of helpful information. do you have a future project you wish to discuss?"

You could also end the above with the standard "would you have some time in the next week or two?"

If they say "no."

"That's fine, don't want to bug you, but obviously we do a lot of home improvements. Is there a better time you might suggest we call you back?"

They tell you.

" Happy to call you then. Is there a particular reason that is a better time to call you?"

They answer.

"Thankyouverymuchcallyouthen." Click

Shorter script for this offering

"Hi, this is Joanna from Buildit Builders. We have been doing business in the area for 40 years and earned an A+ Better Business Bureau rating. Would you like to get a quote and some choices on an upcoming home improvement project?"

Another script variation

"Hi, this is Joanna from the Buildit company. If you

have a siding, roofing or home improvement project we would like to provide you information on your choices and a quote. We have been in business 40 years and earned an A+ better business rating. There is no obligation and you will get a lot of helpful information. Is there anything we might help you with in the future."

If they say they can't afford anything

"We understand. We do so many projects locally that we are able to offering some financing programs that many have found make the difference. If you have a project you want done one of our home improvement professionals could discuss the project with you and explain some financing options if you wish. Again, there is no obligation and many find the information helpful. Would you have some time in the next week or so?"

For more articles, script samples and audio tips
you can download check out
AccordingToScott.com/script-extras

Summary

You Have to Believe In Something

These script concepts and structures should drive your word choices as you try to set sales appointments.

Don't be part of the "ya, but" crowd that is quick to point out to you that there is an exception to every rule, but doesn't adhere to any rules.

You have mere seconds to say the words that will lead to your business objective. Choosing those words from all your options may take you hours.

To make the best choices you must develop a confidence in certain principles, and adhere to those principles when making your word choices. Your actions and word choices must be congruent with your beliefs about what will work.

I personally smiled and dialed my way to setting more than 2,000 high-level sales appointments in many diverse industries.

In this book you have the drivers of the script components of that success.

Use them and you will set more appointments.

In my experience, many capable salespeople lose out on opportunities, not because of ability or lack of knowledge, but because they lack structure.

It is my hope that this primer has provided a structure toward a systematic approach to best communicating your value and reaching your business objectives.

Stick with this structure and work congruent to the concepts presented and you will set more qualified sales appointments.

Good luck. If you or your sales team need some help contact to discuss your situation and some options.

Scott Channell

www.AccordingToScott.com

For updates, more script samples, audio you can download and tips.
www.AccordingToScott.com/script-extras

About the Author

Scott Channell is a professional speaker,
sales trainer and executive coach.

For more about Scott and service options go to
AccordingToScott.com

Made in the USA
Middletown, DE
08 December 2015

2691985852R00089